THE SPIRIT OF CHARLES LINDBERGH

To Fred

all the very best

Peter Jly

Aug 16 2003

T. Willard Hunter

Charles A. Lindbergh
May. 27, 1927

THE SPIRIT OF CHARLES LINDBERGH

Another Dimension

T. Willard Hunter

Madison Books

Published by Madison Books
4720 Boston Way
Lanham, Maryland 20706

Distributed by National Book Network

The paper used in this publication meets the minimum
requirements of American National Standard for
Information Sciences—Permanence of Paper for
Printed Library Materials, ANSI Z39.48–1984. ♾™
Manufactured in the United States of America.

Library of Congress Cataloging-in-Publication Data

Hunter, T. Willard.
The spirit of Charles Lindbergh : another
dimension / T. Willard Hunter.
p.   cm.
Includes bibliographical references and index.
1. Lindbergh, Charles A. (Charles Augustus),
1902–1974.   2. Air pilots—United
States—Biography.   I. Title.
TL540.L5H86   1993
629.13'092—dc20   92–42418 CIP
[B]

ISBN 1–56833–016–2 (cloth : alk. paper)

Grateful acknowledgment is made for permission to reproduce
the following:

Frontispiece reproduced by permission of National Portrait
Gallery, Smithsonian Institution; Quotation from Frederick
Lewis Allen, Only Yesterday, reprinted by permission
HarperCollins; Letter from Anne Morrow Lindbergh to Ed
and Jeannie Pechin reprinted by permission of Mrs. Lindbergh
and the Pechins.

The Frontispiece

This portrait of a thoughtful young Charles A. Lindbergh appeared on the cover of *Time* announcing the magazine's first Man of the Year. It was drawn five days after the historic trans-Atlantic flight. The artist, Samuel J. Woolf, was invited by a *New York Times* correspondent to go to the American Embassy in Paris for an interview with the new hero. Woolf drew the portrait during that meeting. The artist said the aviator was concerned with finding a suit for his lanky frame, and that he was bewildered by all the fuss about his flight. Woolf observed that the machine was Lindbergh's god, and that he trusted it implicitly. Both artist and pilot signed the drawing, dating it May 27, 1927.

Owned then by *The New York Times*, the portrait was borrowed by *Time* for its January 2, 1928, cover story. Three years later, fifteen anonymous well-wishers presented the portrait as a gift to the German-town Friends School in Philadelphia, where it hung in the history department for over fifty years. In 1987, the School forwarded the work on extended loan to the National Portrait Gallery of the Smithsonian Institution in Washington, to be the centerpiece of the *Time* Man of the Year exhibition.

It was almost by accident that *Time* initiated this annual selection, which has become a yearly news event in itself. The fledgling publication had enjoyed phenomenal success since its founding in 1923 by Henry Luce, son of Presbyterian missionaries in China, and Yale classmate Briton Hadden. Each week's front cover featured the foremost news personality of the previous seven days. At the end of December 1927, the editors were reviewing a slow week and were hard pressed to come up with a newsworthy subject. "Forget the man of the week," someone finally suggested. "Let's select a man of the year." For 1927, that choice was easy.

To

Jim and Ellie Newton

who have been a joy and inspiration
to many families

including not only the Lindberghs
but countless Hunter types as well

Contents

Preface xi
Author's Note xiii
Acknowledgments xv
1. The Lindbergh Phenomenon 1
2. Shaping Beliefs 9
3. Uncommon Friends 17
4. The Fifth Dimension 27
5. Nerves of Steel 33
6. The Personal Person 45
7. The Cowboy and the Pilot 55
8. Germany and the Fall from Grace 61
9. Roosevelt and an Achilles Heel 69
10. The Sad Saga of the Press 79
11. Seeds of Trouble 87
12. Don't Call Me—I'll Call You 91
13. Philosophy of Force 95
14. Of Flight and Life 101
15. Great Destiny in the Air—Goal I 103
16. Keep Out of War—Goal II 109
17. Moral Control of Science—Goal III 115
18. The Maui Hideaway 123
19. The Lone Eagle's Last Flight 131
20. Epilogue 141

Appendices
A. Great in Character 145
B. The Aloha Cottage 147
C. The Lindbergh Miracle 149
D. Farewell Address 155
E. Selected Words 157

Bibliography 169

Index 171

Preface

Volumes have been written about Charles A. Lindbergh, the twenty-five-year-old farm boy turned airmail pilot who in May 1927 astounded the world with his daring and meticulously prepared solo flight from New York to Paris. Almost single-handedly, he ushered in the air age. Ever since the Wright Brothers rose from the sands of Kitty Hawk a quarter of a century earlier, increasing numbers of men and women had been entering the air. But it was Lindbergh who swept the world into air consciousness. It was Lindbergh whose name dominated aviation—both commercial and military—until World War II.

Beyond the saturation coverage of his heroic deeds in the air, abundant comment has also been made on his extraordinary contributions to medical research and science; to rocketry and space exploration; to the tragic loss of his firstborn; to his attempts to keep the United States out of World War II, followed by his total dedication to Allied victory; and to his unflagging efforts to preserve the realm of nature and its ability to sustain an adequate quality of life. Yet few know about the famous aviator's basic attitudes. Why did he do what he did? What was his belief system and how did it change? What were his motivations and spiritual dimension? What was his worldview, and what were his concerns about the future of civilization? Is he a prophet for the twenty-first century when he says:

> If we do not control our science by a
> higher moral force, it will destroy us.

We know a great deal about the *Spirit of St. Louis*. We know a great deal less about the spirit of her pilot.

Charles Lindbergh is counted among a significant number of scientists and other leaders who have been convinced that spiritual reality is as authentic as material reality. He was originally influenced toward this view by Alexis Carrel, the Nobel Prize–winning French surgeon. During World War II, U.S. Chief of Staff George C. Marshall declared that Napoleon's axiom, "morale is to materiel as two is to one," had been superseded, and was now more like six to one. One of the most famous scientific predictions of the century came from the electrical "Wizard of Schenectady," Charles Steinmetz, who said, "The next great discovery will be in the realm of the spirit." Charles Lindbergh's basic quest was in search of such a discovery.

xi

Author's Note

This book arose out of a conversation with Reeve Lindbergh, the youngest of Charles and Anne's six children, in Minnesota in 1987. Former Minnesota Governor Elmer L. Andersen, as president of the Charles A. Lindbergh Fund, had begun stressing the importance of recognizing Lindbergh's spiritual side and had instigated the republication of the aviator's testament of faith, *Of Flight and Life.* He believed Minnesota's most famous son should be remembered not only for his aeronautical and scientific contributions, but for his philosophical legacy as well. During the same period, I was lobbying Minnesota officials to expand the content of the flyer's quotations at the base of his statue at the state capitol in Saint Paul, to reflect this wider perspective.

During our conversation, Reeve said that whenever she heard Governor Andersen speak and me talk, she kept thinking there was a book in there somewhere. "Elmer is especially interested," she wrote, "in many of the same elements in my father's thought that have seemed underrepresented to you." I did not think much more about it until the summer of 1988, when I was the closing speaker in Little Falls, Minnesota, at a three day conference of the Charles A. Lindbergh Fund, an organization that addresses the aviator's concern for the balance between science and nature. Following my address, "The Three Goals of Charles A. Lindbergh," Reeve came up to me and said she thought that what I had said was a chapter of the book. This renewed interest started me thinking—and pulling notes together. But the reader must be aware that Reeve bears no responsibility for any of the contents of this book, which is neither collaborative nor "authorized." The reporting and opinions are entirely my own.

Any one who was alive and breathing on May 21, 1927, the day the *Spirit of St. Louis* landed in Paris, is something of an authority on Charles Lindbergh. In addition to this qualification, I have had a number of lifetime encounters with the man himself, both indirectly and personally. Indirectly, I grew up in his home state of Minnesota and quite probably saw him in a pasture outside Northfield where two pilots were offering rides. Lindbergh did in fact make a barnstorming swing through the southern part of the state in the summer of 1923. In 1927 my family and I were on hand, with 10,000 other highly excited people, at the Wold Chamberlain Field between Minneapolis and Saint Paul on a hot August day when the *Spirit of St. Louis* touched down there on the forty-eight-state welcome-home tour. I will never forget an unshaven man working the crowd with an armful of banners crying, "Pennant, souvenir of Lindbergh—he done it!" That summer I saw his boyhood home on the Mississippi and the wreckage done to it by no-doubt well-meaning fans.

Personally, I had several conversations with the man by virtue of my friendship with his most intimate friend, Jim Newton. My wife Mary Louise and I first met the Lindberghs with the Newtons on the island of Captiva in Florida, where Anne was writing what was to become a durable classic, *Gift From the Sea*. My next encounter was at Jim and Ellie Newton's wedding in Washington during World War II. Charles was best man, and I was enlisted to be his chauffeur for his return to the Army Navy Club. In 1951 I had some conversations with him at the Shoreman Hotel. Following his death, I came to know him in an interesting way following a professional assignment on Maui. The Minnesota Historical Society asked me to stay on and conduct oral-history interviews with friends of the Lindberghs in Hawaii.

In a way Lindbergh has been a lifelong study for me. For example, I helped Jim Newton with his book *Uncommon Friends,* which recounts his thirty-six year friendship with Lindbergh. I have been active in the Charles A. Lindbergh Fund since 1977 and was a member of the International Committee for the celebration in France of the sixtieth anniversary of the New York-to-Paris flight.

In addition to all that, I lived through the Lindbergh era. Like so many of my time, I could not avoid being shaped by the ambience he helped create.

Acknowledgments

This book is dedicated to Jim and Ellie Newton of Fort Myers Beach, Florida. The Newtons and the Hunters have been friends for over fifty years. Although Jim has reviewed the manuscript and made helpful recommendations, the opinions expressed herein do not necessarily reflect his perspective, which he brilliantly recorded in his own work, *Uncommon Friends*.

It has been a special treat for me to come to know Reeve Lindbergh Tripp. Although she is not to be held responsible for the contents of this book, it never would have been started but for her. She kindly reviewed the manuscript and made astute and beneficial comments.

Bruce L. Larson, Minnesota historian and biographer of Lindbergh's father, has contributed important observations, especially in reference to the family's heritage.

Lee Merrell, my Philadelphia sister-in-law, and neighbor Ed Doty reviewed the manuscript and came through with perceptive perspectives.

Judith Ann Schiff, chief archivist at Yale University Library and special archivist of the Lindbergh collection there, has been a good friend and helpful tipster, even though prior commitments to other writers precluded my access to the Yale stacks. The aviator had total confidence in Judy's stewardship of his letters and memorabilia, and she was coeditor of his posthumously published *Autobiography of Values*. I was pleased to have a part in arranging with Larry Pryor for the deposit at Yale of the considerable correspondence between his father, Samuel F. Pryor Jr., and Charles A. Lindbergh.

Appreciation goes to Lori Ives of Claremont, who in the 1980s published my communications newsletter *Words*. She and her assistant, Peggy Zappen, have been indeed patient in preparing the manuscript for publication.

The editor of this work is Claudia Suzanne of Orange, California, who chiseled, honed, and enhanced it with great competence and grace.

Mary Louise, my ever-loving wife, has been most supportive and forbearing. There is now another star in her crown.

Claremont, California, 1993

xv

"You and I can take hard knocks," my father said before I was half-way through grade school. "We'll get along no matter what happens."

Our short-term survival may depend upon the knowledge of atomic scientists and the performance of supersonic aircraft. Our long-term survival depends, alone, on the character of man.

Our salvation, and our only salvation, is to control the arm of western science by the mind of a western philosophy guided by the eternal truths of God.

1

The Lindbergh Phenomenon

It was the love of flying primarily, and secondarily the hope of advancing aviation's development, that caused me to make the New York–to–Paris flight with my Spirit of St. Louis in 1927.

The Lindbergh phenomenon may be unexplainable. There was something about the man himself that exploded in the public mind: there has been nothing like it before or since.

Here was a largely self-educated farm youngster, the only child of estranged parents, a college dropout. His father was an immigrant from Sweden who became a controversial United States congressman. As a teenager, the young man ran a 120-acre farm by himself for two years on the banks of the upper Mississippi. Throughout his amazing career, he never followed a pattern.

How does a Charles Lindbergh rise from the soil of Minnesota and shift the world? What combination of genes, chromosomes, air, water, quirks of history, states of art, upbringing, boyhood environment, role models—destiny itself, the brooding of God—throws onto the path of history such a personality? How does a Shakespeare happen? Or a Mozart? Or Will Rogers? Winston Churchill? Martin Luther King?

Lindbergh was not, after all, the first to fly the Atlantic. The U.S. Navy managed to get a four-engine biplane from Newfoundland to the Azores in 1919. Five weeks later, British aviators John Alcock and Arthur Brown flew the two thousand miles from Newfoundland to Ire-

1

land. Why did Lindbergh cause the explosion? It had nothing to do with artificial hype; perhaps that was what was so dramatic about it. He never did anything to promote himself, or the public's reaction to him. His appeal lay not so much in what he did as in what he was.

One writer recounted that on May 20, "No sooner had the word been flashed along the wires that Lindbergh had started than the whole population of the country became united in the exaltation of a common emotion." That evening, when forty thousand boxing fans were waiting in Yankee Stadium for the Maloney-Sharkey fight to start, the announcer got them on their feet, asking them to pray for Lindbergh. Young Jimmy Stewart, who years later was to play the lead in the movie about the flight, celebrated his nineteenth birthday that day. On sick leave from Princeton, he made models of the *Spirit of St. Louis* and of the Eiffel Tower. Setting these up in the display window of his father's hardware store in Indiana, Pennsylvania, young Stewart inched the plane toward the tower as the reports came in.

Will Rogers wrote in his May 20, 1927, column:

No attempt at jokes today. A slim, tall, bashful, smiling American boy is somewhere over the middle of the Atlantic Ocean where no lone human being has ever ventured before. He is being prayed for to every kind of Supreme Being that has a following. If he is lost, it will be the most universally regretted single loss we ever had. But that kid ain't going to fail.

Frederick Lewis Allen, longtime editor of *Harper's* magazine, tried to explain the outpouring of emotion in his popular evaluation of the 1920s, *Only Yesterday:*

Why this idolization of Lindbergh? The explanation is simple. A disillusioned nation fed on cheap heroics and scandal and crime was revolting against the low estimate of human nature which it had allowed itself to entertain. For years the American people had been spiritually starved. Something that people needed, if they were to live at peace with themselves and with the world, was missing from their lives.

And all at once Lindbergh provided it. Romance, chivalry, self-dedication—here they were, embodied in a modern Galahad for a generation which had forsworn Galahads. Lindbergh did not accept the moving-picture offers that came his way, he did not sell testimonials, did not boast, did not get himself involved in scandal, conducted himself with unerring taste—and was handsome and brave withal. The machinery of ballyhoo was ready and waiting to lift him up where every eye could see him. Is it any wonder that the public's reception of him took on the aspects of a vast religious revival?

Pretty good, one reflects, for a stunt flyer. But also, one must add, pretty good for the American people. They had shown that they had better taste in heroes than anyone would have dared to predict.

This "taste in heroes" was touched on by Will Rogers in an article dated June 5:

Another thing about reading about Lindbergh, the reason that people have eaten it up all this time is because it's the only thing that has been in the papers in years that was clean, and no dirt connected with it in any way. People hadn't read clean stuff in so long they just went crazy over this.

Harvard theologian James Luther Adams has put it simply: "For the time, Lindbergh changed the reputation of human nature."

The man extraordinaire, who in one sweep justified air travel, raised the spirits of people across the world, and gave new meaning to the concepts of romance and decency, was also an ultra American hero. As a boy he lived half the year in an urban environment, the other half on the fading frontier. It was expected he would study in high school, excel in college, and go on to a successful life in engineering. Yet he got through high school by a fluke and washed out of college altogether. At the University of Wisconsin, his only acceptable grades were in rifle and pistol marksmanship. A crack shot, he was reputed to be able to score fifty bull's-eyes in succession. His main ambition was to learn to fly. He had always shunned formal studies, but when told as an army cadet that there were some seventy subjects to master before earning his wings, he buckled down and finished at the top of his class—a beautiful example of motivation as a key to learning. Commissioned on graduation as a second lieutenant in the Army Air Service Reserve, he moved on to barnstorming and the air mail. He later would become a medical researcher, rocketry pioneer, author, and conservationist.

Although he disliked publicity throughout his life, he never stopped attracting it; like a latter-day Midas, everything he touched turned to publicity. He had to work hard not to be in the public eye.

Lindbergh's many accomplishments, too numerous to contain here, are all integral to the Phenomenon. It annoyed him to be boxed into the one event that made him famous. He seldom went out socially, but when he did, he would afterwards complain to his wife Anne, "They always keep flying me to Paris." He felt he had moved beyond Paris. The more people wanted to honor him for ushering in the era of air travel, the less he could tolerate their acclaim. Jimmy Doolittle, a fellow pilot of the early days, tried along with others to persuade Lindbergh to come back from Borneo, where he was saving the rhinoceros, to attend a 1967 recognition banquet in honor of the fortieth anniversary of the Flight. He sent word: "No thanks. I devoted time to that in 1927 and 1928 and wrote two books about it. But this is not that era, and I am not that boy."

He did not, he added, like dressing up in "those awful clothes, eating that bad hotel food, and listening to those dull speeches." Rather, he told Jimmy, he would prefer to meet in a favorite Chinese restaurant in Manhattan so they could visit as two old pilots.

He was urged to run for office—senator from Minnesota, president of the United States. He could have had either office for the asking. In James Thurber's *Carnival,* one character says, "In spite of the nominations, my mother's going to vote for Lindbergh." But politics was not for him.

Even today, the mystique will not quit. A recent national convention of matchbook collectors displayed the "Lindbergh Cover" from a 1927 dinner in New York, which they called "one of the most prized match covers in existence." The *Spirit of St. Louis* is still the most popular exhibit at the Smithsonian Institution in Washington. And out in the

Pacific, although the numbers are diminishing, people for a long time will be visiting his grave on Maui.

The tag "Lucky Lindy" irritated him no end. Many times he said, "Luck had nothing to do with it." What he meant was that the sobriquet trivialized the elements that had contributed to the success of his Flight—the support of the Saint Louis backers, the perseverance and designing genius of the Ryan Company in San Diego, his own training, experience, and hard work, the years of aviation development since Kitty Hawk. He did not reject "Lucky Lindy" because of the moniker's failure to give *him* sufficient credit. The catchy headline, along with "Flying Fool," sounded to him like the familiar daredevil stereotype of the early aviators, when his real aim was to position aviation in the public mind as an acknowledged, practical means of transportation for everybody. His first book about the Flight, after all, was entitled *We,* and by that he did not mean only "me and my plane." He was including the teams in Saint Louis and San Diego that had put him into the plane. His friend Jim Newton says he was well aware that he was "standing on the shoulders of giants."

Then too, Lindbergh's luck was not always good. He had more than his share of tragedy and difficulty. Yet during his career, if it was not luck, there was something like it that seemed to surround him. A guardian angel? Providence? The number of crashes he walked away from is incredible. During his days as a flying cadet he survived a midair collision, and by the time he had added some airmail experience, he had become the first pilot in the United States ever to make four emergency jumps from a plane, gaining him an early membership in the parachuters' Caterpillar Club, so named for the silkworm that was responsible for the fabric. On two of these jumps, he was almost killed by his abandoned plane circling toward him in descent. While much of his endurance and survival can be attributed to his cutting the odds by careful advance attention to details, it did seem as though an impressive something else was going for him as well. A retired navigator who has researched the century's weather history over the north Atlantic has said that conditions on May 20–21, 1927, were more favorable than at any other time in fifty years. Indeed, when Admiral Richard E. Byrd flew the same pattern a mere six weeks later, he was unable to land in Paris because of a storm over the city and had to turn back and land in the water on the French coast. If this had happened to Lindbergh, the Phenomenon would look quite different. And what kind of luck was it that captured the hearts of so many French people who thought he had named his plane for their beloved royal saint, Louis IX?

Certainly he was lucky in love: he and Anne lived one of the great love stories of the century—and one of the most complex. Both would probably say it was more fate than luck. But even beyond that, good fortune appeared sometimes to envelop all that he touched. In November 1982, for example, the pilot's old Curtiss Jenny, a JN-4D World War I biplane he had flown in barnstorming days, was on display at the Minneapolis Northwestern National Bank when a Thanksgiving weekend fire destroyed the building. In the midst of the wreckage, the plane was unscathed.

It could be argued that even some of the negatives became positive: the tragedy of the separation of Lindbergh's parents when he was a boy, the enforced loneliness of his early years, the insecurity of being uprooted twice a year from two distantly separate domiciles, the fact that he was never allowed to finish a normal school year—even this became a "lucky" force for him, creating the extreme individualism necessary to his destiny. If he had played end on the high school football team, or danced up a storm at the senior prom, he might have drifted off into obscure pursuits. Alden Whitman of *The New York Times* speculated that Lindbergh the boy saw in the plane that flew up the river a hope for escaping youthful unhappiness. Lindbergh, however, always wrote of his childhood in idyllic terms.

Some said his good fortune came partly from his extraordinarily handsome appearance. His commanding, six-feet-three presence—"Slim" the pilots called him—could hardly have been expected from the genes. He was the first on either side of his family in three generations to reach six feet. He had big, Swedish farmer's hands, acute blue eyes, a smile that lit up the front pages, extraordinary mechanical aptitude, nerves of steel, and a phenomenal memory. Were there also propitious genes passed down from ancient Vikings who conquered trackless oceans? With his natural endowments, set in motion by determination and hard work, coupled with his descent from the clouds where the gods live, his appeal was simply more than most people could be expected to withstand.

He might have been pleased with not quite so much luck. Perhaps he would have had less trouble with press and public if he had been a short, fat, bald, cigar-chomping, hell-raising grease monkey. But he was what he was—a singular combination of good fortune, dedicated performance, unaffected personality, and genuine character, who in an "accident" of timing arrived front and center just when technology promised a bright future for humankind by making possible a glamorous mode of travel in the skies. "I was astonished at the effect my successful landing in France had on the nations of the world," he wrote. "To me, it was like a match lighting a bonfire."

Some match. Some bonfire.

2

Shaping Beliefs

To me in youth, science was more important than either man or God.

Charles Lindbergh was a second-generation Swedish immigrant. This reality shaped much of his life and beliefs. He had an immigrant's intense patriotism. When World War II loomed and he wanted to keep America out of it, he called up an immigrant's argument, "We came here to escape Europe's ceaseless wars. Why should we now go back in?"

His father, Charles August Lindbergh, born in Stockholm, January 20, 1859, was brought that year from Skåne, Sweden, to the New World by his parents, August, 50, and Louise, 20.

In Sweden this couple had been known as Ola and Louisa Mansson. Ola had served as an influential reform member of the Riksdag, the Swedish parliament, from 1847 to 1858. A combination of political and financial troubles made him decide to start afresh in America. Apparently he thought a new name should be part of the new life, so he changed his from Ola Mansson to August Lindbergh. August was a name often used by Swedish royalty; "Lindbergh" was a combination of words from nature meaning, roughly, "wooded mountain." Their new baby, Charles August, was named in honor of Crown Prince Charles, a friend of Mansson who the same year became King Charles XV.

In that era, Minnesota was known as The Glorious New Scandinavia, with more Swedes emigrating there than to any other state. Between 1845 and 1930, one and a quarter million Swedes came to the

9

New World in five waves. In 1859, the Lindberghs were a part of the second. Although the Statue of Liberty and Ellis Island were not yet part of the scene, the current Immigration Museum on the Island features the Lindberghs as one of many representative American immigrant families of the nineteenth century.

The Lindberghs' arduous trip was typical—six weeks on the high seas from Sweden to New York, long train rides to Dubuque, Iowa, and a river boat up the Mississippi to Minneapolis–Saint Paul. Finally, a westbound ox-cart prairie schooner took them to Stearns County, where they settled on the south bank of the Sauk River, near Melrose. Although nearby Sauk Center would be made famous by Sinclair Lewis's *Main Street,* the Lindbergh family home at that time was, according to biographer Bruce L. Larson, "literally on the edge of the frontier." It was a place where "immigrants regularly stopped . . . on their journeys north and west into Minnesota and the Dakotas . . . The warm hospitality of August and Louisa was widely known."

August, a natural leader with long political experience in Sweden, became town clerk, village recorder, justice of the peace, and postmaster in the new community. It was not surprising that his son Charles August naturally edged toward politics. Like his father in the Old World, the son became a controversial legislator in the New, serving Minnesota's Sixth District in the United States House of Representatives from 1907 to 1917. Before he became a congressman, he and his second wife, Evangeline Land Lindbergh, in naming their only child, who was to become an apolitical aviator, reverted to the Swedish royal "Charles Augustus." Although the father's and son's names were, in fact, technically different, they were nevertheless referred to as "Senior" and "Junior." The younger's firstborn, the child who was kidnapped, was, in turn, named Charles Augustus Lindbergh, and was also referred to as "Junior."

Walter S. Ross in *The Last Hero* (Harper, 1968) notes:

The character of Charles A. Lindbergh clearly reproduces many traits found in his father and grandfather. The Lindbergh men all display the same hard, central sense of purpose, the same fearless, even foolhardy, independence of mind and action. In different countries, in different centuries, there is something unchanging, refractory, defiant, even downright cussed, in this family. One is not usually afforded such an uncluttered view of repeated cause and effect in real life.

The established state church of Sweden was Lutheran. Consequently, August (nee Ola) and Louise (nee Louisa) would surely have been baptized in infancy as a matter of course and registered in the Swedish Lutheran church. Many Swedes who came to the New World, perhaps because of the rigorous demands of the frontier, took their Lutheranism more seriously than those who stayed behind. It is not clear how much this was true of the transplanted Lindberghs, but what is clear is that the aviator's father grew up in a home where the atmosphere was warm, close-knit, and social and where the Bible and a history of the world were the two most frequently used volumes. There are other clues to the family's religious leanings, as well. For example, when August severed his right arm in an accident at the local mill, which turned out to require amputation, the family called first for the Rev. C. S. Harrison. The doctor was thirty miles away. While the pastor was, of course, no surgeon, he was obviously sought for family support and as an intermediary to other services. In a community of relocated Swedes, the cleric's denomination was almost certainly Lutheran.

Years later, Congressman Lindbergh, who was known as "C.A." because of the way he signed his name, would be influenced by the lectures of John Dietrich, minister of the First Unitarian Church in Minneapolis, and would himself join that denomination, noted for its intellectual emphasis. (Dietrich would later conduct the congressman's funeral in Minneapolis.) Bruce L. Larson in *Lindbergh of Minnesota* notes that C.A. "was not inclined to follow the regular patterns of organized religion. But he did believe in God. Significantly, the largest single element in the Lindbergh library was made up of books on evolution and the related debate between science and religion."

Carl Bolander, a builder and real estate partner of the congressman's, described a drive he and C.A. made into the lake country north of Little Falls. They stopped on a hill and in silence viewed a lake and a yellow road winding through the pines. After viewing the scene for a time, Lindbergh broke the silence "with an outburst of such eloquence and impassioned feeling that I'd never heard from him before," Bolander said.

> Some men tell us there is no God, or that God is a puny crea-
> ture shut up in churches and creeds! I need no scientific
> analysis or theological arguments to show me the reality of the
> bigness of *my* God when I look at this!

On the family's distaff side, C. A.'s first wife, Mary LaFond, whose father was editor of the *Little Falls Transcript,* came from a French-Canadian Irish family. They were among the original settlers of the Minnesota town in the 1850s and were presumably Roman Catholic. Mary, however, became an active member of the Congregational Church in Little Falls. One of the two daughters from the Lindbergh-LaFond union, Eva Lindbergh Spaeth, lived to be lifetime friends with her half-brother, Charles.

C.A.'s second wife, Evangeline Land Lindbergh, the aviator's mother, was denominationally unattached and much oriented toward science. In 1898, she earned the Bachelor of Science degree from the University of Michigan, where she was said to have been the prettiest girl on campus. Her mother was a Lodge, and two of her Lodge uncles were physicians. Evangeline's grandfather, Edwin Albert Lodge, was a doctor-turned–Baptist minister who preached fiery sermons in a wooden country church on the shores of Michigan's Orchard Lake and baptized converts in the cold water. Apparently his granddaughter was not one of them.

The Lands were a scientific family. Evangeline's father, Dr. Charles H. Land, was a dentist and the inventor of the porcelain crown. He had a substantial laboratory in his combined residence-office in Detroit. During the Lindberghs' extended stopovers twice a year when they transferred between Washington and Little Falls, young Charles spent many a fascinated day at the Lands', learning science on his own. "There," he wrote, "I could rob the icebox, melt lead, bake clay, draw wire, mix explosives, make electric batteries, turn out brass cannon on a lathe—carrying out the more dangerous activities under my grandfather's or my uncle's direction. I decided I would become an engineer."

The debate between science and religion, which so interested C. A., became a subject of national discussion in the early twentieth century. Young Charles found one side to have the more compelling argument:

> As I lost confidence in the Bible, I gained confidence in science. . . . To me in youth, science was more important than either man or God. The one I took for granted; the other was too intangible for me to understand. . . . Like most modern youth, I worshiped science.

Widower C.A., successful lawyer and real-estate-developer, was apparently accustomed to going to church, probably with his first wife, whom he had lost two years before the attractive twenty-four-year-old Evangeline Land arrived in Little Falls to teach high school chemistry in the autumn of 1900. She happened to room at the Antlers Hotel, where C.A. was staying. Their rooms had windows facing each other for "easily arranged signals," Evangeline recalled. They became friends walking the same street to work. In a letter to her mother in Detroit about their budding romance, Evangeline wrote, "The widower walked home from church this morning with me and another girl." C.A. and Evangeline were married in Detroit in March 1901.*

The early family atmosphere was not such as to encourage religious inclination. His father did not talk about it, and his mother was pretty much all science. "My mother read the Bible to me," Charles wrote in his memoirs, "but explained that no one knew how much of it was true." His church encounters were negative, and he regarded attendance as "an

---

*Although young Charles was born in Detroit, he is sometimes called a native of Minnesota. He was known to refer to himself that way. The Detroit birth came about because Evangeline preferred the care available through her Michigan family of medical professionals to the rudimentary facilities of rural Minnesota. Before the baby was due, she boarded a train for Detroit. Soon after, she returned to Little Falls.

Years later, when visiting with friends one evening at the old farm house on the upper Mississippi, Charles was including himself among the Minnesota natives present. Someone objected, "But you were born in Detroit, weren't you?"

"Yes," Lindbergh replied, "but that's not what's important. What's important is that I got started in Minnesota."

ordeal to be cautiously avoided." Decades later, he wrote in *Autobiography of Values* of an incident when he was four years old:

> The first serious assertion of independence I remember was in going to church. That was when my father ran for Congress for the first time. Apparently it was desirable for a candidate's family to be seen in church. At least my mother thought so. . . . This seemed to me such an unpleasant and unnecessary experience that I marshaled all the forces at my command against it. I revolted so effectively that I was never taken to church again, but the incident left me a skeptic toward religion, questioning the beneficence of God.

This would seem a rather impressive conclusion for a four-year-old to make, based on one summer's hour in church. At least he was consistent. His skinny dipping boyhood friend Alex Johnson repeatedly invited Charles to go with him to Sunday School. The answer was always no. He did not speak—even at age seven, eight, or nine—of skepticism toward religion or of questioning the beneficence of God. He just said no. Going into buildings with other people would never be a high priority.

He called his church experience not only "unpleasant," but "unnecessary." The "unnecessary" test was to be a Lindbergh trademark. Aboard the *Spirit of St. Louis* he permitted himself nothing unnecessary. He clipped off the edges of maps to avoid unnecessary weight. In school and college, he felt it was unnecessary to study anything outside his current concern. Church was unnecessary. In his final Maui days, he wanted nothing unnecessary done for him. He was quite capable of deciding for himself—from age four on—what was necessary and what was not. The church anecdote also anticipates Lindbergh's consistent dedication to his personal interests. As an only child he was used to getting his own way. At four, he could hardly be expected to think that his own discomfort for an hour in church might be a price he could lovingly pay to help his parents, whether politically motivated or not. But throughout his days, he was clear as to the quality of life that he personally preferred.

His childhood reaction was not the final word on Lindbergh's church attendance, however. Although, he stayed away, with few lifetime exceptions, he chose in the end to be laid to rest in a quiet spot beside a country church.

Precursors of his later faith appeared in his youth. "I do not recall how the concept of God formed in my mind," he wrote, "any more than I can recall learning to speak and understand the English language." And although he claimed that in his younger years he did not believe in anything except the material, he said in Paris after the flight, "A kind Providence placed me in Ambassador [Myron T.] Herrick's hands." In his Pulitzer Prize-winning account of the trans-Atlantic flight he wrote:

> It's hard to be an agnostic up here in the *Spirit of St. Louis*. If one dies, all this goes on existing in a plan so perfectly balanced, so wonderfully simple, so incredibly complex that it's far beyond our comprehension—worlds and moons revolving; planets orbiting on suns; suns flung with apparent recklessness through space. There's the infinite magnitude of the universe; there's the infinite detail of its matter—the outer star, the inner atom. And man conscious of it all—a worldly audience to what if not to God?

This is indeed a classic statement of a faith arising from the intricate interdependence of creation. Lindbergh is not the only one who, after such observation, has concluded that it takes quite some faith to be an atheist. Yet one wonders whether the twenty-five-year-old pilot had actually reached such a judgment. Persons close to the family are inlined to believe these sentiments were probably closer to those he held at age fifty than at twenty-five. But it is true he was always aware of the mystery of the so-called "fifth dimension" of reality. With some courage, he revealed he had experienced ghostlike companions in the *Spirit of St. Louis*. And he told his friend Jim Newton, "If you commit yourself to something fully, unseen forces come to your aid."

These formative concepts were to flower into something more significant in later years, particularly in the profound shift his thinking took during the war and beyond.

3

Uncommon Friends

In Carrel, spiritual and material values were met and blended as in no other man I knew.

Outside of his own remarkable self-development techniques, and his exceptional wife, Anne, the most important influences on the spiritual growth of the adult Charles Lindbergh were two of his best friends. One was a world-famous research surgeon, author, and Nobel laureate, Alexis Carrel. The other was a dynamic businessman, counselor, and raconteur, a man Anne Lindbergh says has a genius for friendship—Jim Newton. There were very few people on the planet to whom Lindbergh gave his confidence. These two were among them.

Nearly everyone can tell you that Charles Lindbergh flew the ocean. Very few are aware that he was also a foremost medical researcher who constructed a heart perfusion pump that ultimately led to heart bypass surgery. This he accomplished with Alexis Carrel.

Lindbergh's interest in the problem was engaged by way of his wife's older sister. Elisabeth suffered a cardiac complication her doctor said was incurable and inoperable. The heart could not be stopped long enough for repair without starving the other organs of blood. To Lindbergh this looked like an engineering problem. Surely, he thought, someone must have constructed or was constructing an artificial heart to circulate the blood during an operation. After many fruitless inquiries, he

17

was finally referred to Alexis Carrel. The great French surgeon and his wife were binational, spending three months each summer in France and the other nine months in New York, where he was directing research in the Department of Experimental Surgery at the Rockefeller Institute for Medical Research. Lindbergh was introduced to him there.

In 1912 Alexis Carrel had become the first, and for a long time the only, surgeon to win a Nobel Prize. The award came for his method of suturing small blood vessels during surgery and for work in transplanting organs. According to Ross, the surgeon was so adroit with his hands that within the thickness of a piece of paper he could make tiny stitches that could hardly be seen from either side. In the 1930s, his writings made him famous. His bestseller, *Man the Unknown,* owed much of its popularity to the author's articulate skill in emphasizing the supremacy of the qualitative over the quantitative, and of the spiritual over the material. He was able to position the big ideas in language appealing to the modern, science-oriented reader. Also during this period, a popular series of articles by Carrel on health-related subjects appeared in *Reader's Digest,* with such titles as "Breast Feeding," "Work in the Laboratory of Your Private Life," "Married Love," and "Prayer is Power." His collected works reside in Georgetown University, Washington, D.C.

When Lindbergh explained his interest in heart surgery, the French specialist was, of course, intrigued. He soon determined that the young celebrity's ambitious proposal was serious and potentially beneficial. He himself had begun preliminary work on a possible pump, but he was now working on other commitments. He could, however, provide office and laboratory space, get the newcomer started, and periodically consult on progress.

Not only did the two become warm friends from the outset; there was an unusual chemistry about two such names working together on such a project. They managed secrecy for years, and when the announcement of their perfusion pump came, it was big news. The breakthrough was first reported in *Science* magazine in June 1935. Upon the publication of their book, *The Culture of Organs,* the two men were featured on the front cover of *Time* in June 1938. They had produced a perfusion pump that could keep organs alive outside the body while the natural heart was being repaired and that ultimately led to a mechanical heart. The press dubbed it the "Lindbergh Heart." It came too late to save Elisabeth Morrow, but untold numbers of bypass beneficiaries since then can be grateful to the Lone Eagle. Although modern procedures are, to be sure, more sophisticated, Lindbergh and Carrel started the process.

The two men and their wives were lifelong friends. *Time's* cover story commented on their living as neighbors during the summers of 1937 and 1938 on the Brittany Islands of Saint Gildas and Illiec off the northwest coast of France. The article concluded:

> It makes an arresting picture—two men, one an ageless seer, the other a young and devoted inventor, sitting on two rocks in the middle of a sea, talking and planning ways to prolong the life and end the ills of mankind.

From the beginning of their association, Carrel was clearly impressed with the brilliance and dedication of the self-taught junior scientist now under his tutelage. The feeling was mutual, as Lindbergh was to say that the surgeon had "the most stimulating mind I have ever met." The Frenchman's medical genius and the American's engineering skill made a winning combination. But the older man sensed there was something missing in the younger; and what he thought was missing was the spiritual dimension. To help him in this area, he called on Jim Newton. The doctor wanted the businessman to explain how he had found a faith.

Jim Newton was born in Philadelphia of a physician father and a "125 percent Irish" mother. A bright and curious high school kid, he took over the family basement to become one of the city's foremost ham radio operators. His parents enrolled him at Dartmouth, but he chucked that to explore the West as a hobo cowboy. Returning east after a year, he slipped into sales, which is like saying a duck slips into water. He has always been able to sell just about anything to just about anyone. There is no record that he ever sold a refrigerator to an eskimo, but the over-sight can be explained: (a) his exacting ethical code would be in the way; and (b) he never met an eskimo.

As a teenager he went to work for the Belber Luggage Company and was so successful with the company's New England territory that he was put in charge of eight Southern states. When he arrived in Florida in the mid-1920s and saw the dazzling opportunities in the land boom, he jettisoned the luggage and plunged into real estate development. He was twenty years old. His first project was Edison Park, which occupied select acreage in a residential area of Fort Myers, across the street from the home in which Thomas and Mina Edison had spent fifty winters. The hard-working young man with the million-dollar personality captivated the Edisons, who virtually adopted him and included him in their circle of famous wintertime visitors. Consequently, he became good friends also with auto maker Henry Ford and rubber pioneer Harvey Firestone.

Firestone hired Jim, then twenty-three, took him to Akron as his personal assistant, and immediately started grooming him for the presidency of the Firestone Tire and Rubber Company. After eight years of top positions in real estate and sales, the young executive wondered whether such a pressure-cooker existence was a good idea. He decided to take a year's leave of absence to sort things out. At the end of the year, he was convinced he was meant to concentrate on the human element in industry on a general basis, rather than with just one company. He determined to dedicate his life to bringing a new spirit into every situation he could. The most effective instrument he saw for such an effort was the worldwide program of the Oxford Group, a movement for personal, industrial, and national revitalization. It was later known as Moral Re-Armament (MRA)*. In his earlier luggage salesman days,

---

*Moral Re-Armament (MRA) is a world program of personal and national renewal based on moral standards and the guidance of God. Its success in producing industrial and international teamwork resulted in the program's initiator, Frank Buchman, being nominated twice in the 1950s for the Nobel Peace Prize. Before 1938, the program was known as the Oxford Group. In the 1930s problem drinkers, who were reoriented through its outreach in New York and Akron, developed Alcoholics Anonymous. Co-founders Bill Wilson and Bob Smith, who initially were part of the Oxford Group, codified its life-changing principles into Twelve Steps before separating from the parent movement in the late 1930s. Hundreds of societies have adopted these principles. They are the guidelines of most recovery centers, including those modeled on Minnesota's Hazelden Foundation, such as the Betty Ford Center in Palm Springs and the Hanley-Hazelden Clinic in West Palm Beach. The Twelve Steps involve admitting the need for help; turning over one's life to the care of a higher power, who is then asked to remove one's listed shortcomings; admitting wrongs out loud to somebody; making restitution to those harmed; working at prayer and meditation; and passing the experience on.

Newton had experienced an unexpected redirection in his life through this group. He figured the same principles he was working on, like increased honesty and concern for others, might help bring more teamwork into industrial and community relations. From 1936 on, he was to give most of his time to the program for a quarter of a century, returning to his home in Fort Myers Beach in 1967 at age sixty-two to fashion southwest Florida's leading real estate operation.

During his sabbatical from Firestone, which turned out to be permanent, Newton saw the possibilities of using his talents and experience in industry to help bring a new spirit to businesses and labor unions around the world. In reconciling opposing interests, he was particularly effective with an idea he picked up from a Los Angeles meat packer, Paul Cornelius: "It's not who's right, but what's right."

Jim helped develop a team of businessmen in New York to help solve difficult situations. One of his new colleagues, Ed Moore, had engaged Alexis Carrel in correspondence. Carrel was interested in what Moore was saying about God and God's impact on people. He invited Moore to have a talk. Ed enlisted Jim to accompany him. A lifelong friendship began.

It was 1937. Newton was thirty-two, Carrel sixty-four. At one of their early meetings, Jim shared his personal story of finding a new direction in life. The surgeon said, "Half my age, and you've already learned a great truth—that man does not live by bread alone. Nor does society. It needs equilibrium between material and spiritual nourishment." Carrel was intrigued with the idea of a person experiencing a change of motives and attitudes. He, too, had a lifetime interest in encounters between the transcendental and the human condition, so he was particularly interested in Jim Newton's personal story. He believed Charles Lindbergh would profit from hearing it.

Charles and Anne had been living in self-imposed exile in Europe since 1935. Charles did, however, manage secret return visits to take care of necessary matters and to report to the American government on the reconnaissance they had commissioned him to make respecting the German arms build-up. Early in 1938, Carrel told Newton, "Charles Lindbergh is back for a short time in America . . . I'd like you two to meet . . . I want you to tell him how God came into your life. He and I have talked about these things. He respects my beliefs, but I don't think he's found a satisfying faith himself yet. Possibly you can help him."

The three met at a small French restaurant in Manhattan. Jim hardly had time to become adjusted to sitting down at an intimate table with the world's most famous celebrity, when Carrel moved directly to the point. "Jeem," he said in his pronounced French accent, "tell the kullinel about that experience of yours on that skiing weekend."

Jim told Lindbergh that as a teenage luggage salesman in the early 1920s in New England, he had found himself one weekend at the Toy Town Tavern, a winter resort hotel in Winchendon, Massachusetts. Thinking he was going to a dance, he missed the turn and fell in with a roomful of college students attending a houseparty. They were experimenting with the Oxford Group's popular renewal program which, among other things, emphasized admitting one's own faults instead of spotlighting the other person's, along with such concepts as "there's enough for everyone's need, but not for everyone's greed." In the twenties, the movement was gaining momentum on eastern campuses in the United States as well as at Oxford University (hence the Oxford Group).

Impressed with the freshness and sense of direction apparent in the folks at the houseparty, Jim decided to skip the dance—a resolution aided by the fact that girls who had caught his eye in the dining room as prospective dance partners were in fact part of the gathering into which he had fallen. He was fascinated by the freedom with which the college kids talked about life in general and their own lives in particular, peppered with humorously honest first-person anecdotes. He asked one of the party how a person went about getting hold of their attractive lifestyle. He was told about standards like honesty, purity, unselfishness, and love—plus making a habit of listening to the creative force for direction.

The young salesman asked, "If I make a decision for that tonight, what will I have to do tomorrow?" "I don't know," was the response, "but if tonight you make that decision, tomorrow morning *you'll* know." Jim was impressed that his new friend declined to give a prepackaged answer and decided to try it. If it didn't work, he figured he could always go back to his old ways. For starters, he turned over "as much of my will as I could to as much of God as I understood. I looked up and said, 'You fly it.'"

Carrel was impressed that Jim's new friends had not prescribed procedures or beliefs, but had presented the idea as a scientific experiment, to be given the pragmatic test. He asked what difference it had made in Jim's life. One difference, he said, was getting honest about business practices. Previously, he had shaved the truth and mixed up his money with that of others. His new commitment meant going back to those with whom he had done business, being honest with them, and making restitution. One storekeeper, noting Jim's discomfort in owning up, asked why he was so nervous. "Because," Jim replied, "I was afraid you would lose confidence in me."

"Young man," said the merchant, "you've been honest with me. I'll be honest with you. Up until five minutes ago, I didn't have *any* confidence in you."

A two-pack-a-day smoking habit dropped off. He cleaned up various relationships that were not quite right. He began to treat women differently. He also said he experienced "a new sureness and straightness" in his dealings with people, and noted that taking time each day to be quiet and listen to a power beyond himself had given him a sense of direction he had not known before.

There was something genuine about Jim and his story that won the aviator's confidence right away. It was the beginning of a thirty-six-year friendship that continued until the flyer's death, and still continues with his family. To say Charles Lindbergh was careful about whom he allowed into his tight ring of friends would be a considerable understatement. Within this circle, Jim Newton was probably his most trusted intimate. One evening Charles, Anne, and Jim were standing at the head of the stairs at the Lindbergh home in Darien, Connecticut. The kids had just gone to bed. Charles said quietly, "Jim, if anything should happen to Anne and me . . . would you keep an eye on them?"

In May 1991, from her home in Saint Johnsbury, Vermont, Reeve Lindbergh Tripp, daughter of Charles and Anne, told a reporter about Jim Newton's place in the lives of their family:

We've been such friends for 50 years. He really was, without any question, the closest and most protective friend—in a light and warm and wonderful way—of anyone in my father's life. And he has remained very close to the family. Even now, to the grandchildren and great grandchildren, he's Uncle Jim. He's always been Uncle Jim. He has been a friend to people over and over who have never had many close friends—just like my father. As my mother says, he has a genius for friendship.

Reeve says her parents could completely relax with the Newtons because they knew that what they said would not be in the newspapers the next day.

It would be foolhardy to attempt such a subjective exercise as to identify the precise impact Carrel and Newton had on Charles Lindbergh. The one was a close friend for fourteen years, the other for thirty-six. Carrel, as a scientist, opened for Lindbergh the possibility that the unseen has a great deal more influence on the life of the planet than is generally supposed. But perhaps the tenet of Carrel's that made the greatest impression was:

The quality of life is more important than life itself.

Jim Newton, on the other hand, helped his friend see the great potential in developing human character and relating its improvement to solving social problems and saving the planet. On September 23, 1939, Lindbergh made this diary entry at his home on Long Island:

Jim arrived . . . I invited him to come out to write the Moral Re-Armament article he is planning for *Reader's Digest*. I think he has it in him to do something worthwhile in this line. . . . I am hoping that he may become a strong and constructive force in the religious rejuvenation of this country, and it is essential to help him start in the right way.

Although Newton was the go-between in arranging for the publication of the Carrel health articles in the *Digest* and was on cordial terms with the publisher, DeWitt Wallace, the essay discussed on Long Island was not completed. Both friends were soon caught up in activities related to the developing war.

What is remarkable about the diary entry is that it reveals an entirely new note in Lindbergh's thought processes and shows how far he had come from worshiping science. His proposal of what he thought Jim should write was an ocean's width beyond his earlier reasoning. "The religious rejuvenation of this country" became the core of Lindbergh's remarkable postwar testament of faith, *Of Flight and Life*. It could be argued, although Jim would not initiate such a claim, that the many conversations between the two and with others helped Charles see that a change in human nature could happen, and that if it happened on a large enough scale, it could answer the materialistic science which he saw devastating the world. As he wrote in *Of Flight and Life:*

If we are to keep science from destroying that part of our civilization which is left, if it is to be the great benefit to mankind that we have hoped, we must control it by a philosophy reaching beyond materialism, a philosophy rooted in the character of man and nourished by the eternal truths of God.

Lindbergh was a thoughtful person. As his wife said, he was inner rather than outer directed. It is possible that he could have come to these conclusions by himself. But his judgments might have been quite different if he had never met Alexis Carrel and Jim Newton.

4

The Fifth Dimension

I came to the conclusion that life's greatest values did not lie in results to be obtained through biological mechanics. The longer I live, the more limited I believe rationality to be. I have found that the irrational gives man insight he cannot otherwise attain.

Although Lindbergh was a child of science and knew its power to provide humankind with many needs, he came to see that another dimension was essential. As he moved beyond the worship of science, his life became more oriented toward the unseen. This realm of the spirit is sometimes called the fifth dimension—after length, width, height, and time. As the years rolled by, the aviator-engineer adopted much of Carrel's mysticism and Newton's reliance on "unforeseen forces" for direction. All three believed in extrasensory perception.

He was intrigued by the fact that Carrel was establishing scientific corroboration of medical miracles at Lourdes, France. Cases of ulcers, tuberculosis, bone disease, and cancer "have been almost instantaneously cured at Lourdes," the surgeon had reported.

Lindbergh and Carrel had fellow feelings on general social convictions. They both were concerned, for example, over the flabby morality of America. Also, he found Carrel's mysticism reflected in his own experience. For example, the pilot told his Pan Am associate, Sam Pryor, that on long walks, he often felt he was conversing with his father. In *Autobiography of Values,* he wrote:

27

There are nights when I dream of my father. He appears to me still alive. I see and sense him as clearly as I did before his death. I talk to him from the vantage gained through intervening years, assist him as he once assisted me. I wonder why we have stayed so long apart when we have had such easy access to each other . . . How are we to distinguish the difference between reality and dream?

This interest, along with the reputed spirituality of the East, led Charles and Anne to travel to India from Europe before the war "to study the mystical phenomena so frequently reported as lying beyond conventionally accepted fields of science." On their return he speculated, "Somewhere between the extremes of Western science and Eastern mysticism must lie a better answer than we had yet discovered." He was to pursue balance in this sphere, and in all others, for the rest of his life.

There were other mystical or quasi-mystical leadings. In 1928, the year after the Flight, Lindbergh was making airline surveys in the West. Only twenty-six years old, he felt the pressures and distractions of public acclaim getting to him. At every airport reporters and photographers pushed in. His hotels were watched. There were crowds, headlines, telephone calls, telegrams, interviews, handshaking, backslapping, autographing. His fame was crowding out his life, he felt. Heading over the Great Salt Lake desert one evening, he decided to postpone his next stop and land unscheduled on the sands below. He wanted a little time to himself. Rolling to a stop, he climbed down from the cockpit and walked out into the unspoiled wilderness. "How wonderful to feel and be a part of the desert," he thought. He decided to skip the hotel where he was expected, and spend the night out where no one knew where he was. His thoughts were focused on how to be true to his "core," how to be a "part of the civilization of my time but not to be bound by its conventional superfluity." The desert floor around him was "eroded by stream beds, hemmed by mountains, strewn with cactus, brush, and pebbles." As the stars began coming out, he made a commitment to a change in himself. He would simplify his life. He would no longer allow the environment to control him. To the extent he could, he would take charge, and control his environment.

One decision was seriously to reduce public and organizational activities. He drastically cut down on the number of interviews, ceremonial speeches and dinners, and shunned becoming an officer or director of any company. (He would later make an exception in the case of Pan American World Airways, America First, and a few conservation groups.) Another decision involved the burden of *things*. Like Saint Francis he began to "regard possessions rather as debts than assets." He felt that the concentration required by his work in ideas and research necessitated a tranquility of mind. "I found few ways of gaining such tranquility," he said, "that were more effective than to reduce my possessions."

A third decision related to sleep habits, à la Benjamin Franklin:

As I had stepped up into higher levels of civilized society after my Paris flight, I found that people stayed up smoking, drinking, and talking long after midnight. It was a contagious habit— not the drinking and smoking, for me, because I disliked both— but the staying awake. I always got up the next morning feeling dopey. I decided in the future to go to bed earlier whenever I could break away from a group of people.

It was reminiscent of his forty-eight-state tour of the year before when communities were asked to allow him to turn in early each night.

This wilderness experience held meaning for Lindbergh throughout his life. Years later he said that seeing the beauty of the American Southwest from the air made him understand "why religion owes so much to the desert." A by-product of his determination to simplify his life was discovering the effect of sleep on mental processes. Again exploring realms beyond the rational, he described another road to creativity:

I found that the solutions to current problems in research came most effectively after thought during driving followed by a night's sleep. Obviously some rational process, of which my conscious mind was unaware, took place under such circumstances. Because the results were so consistent, I came to rely on this process. While driving I would consider a problem, then let my mind run free, then consider it again. Before going to sleep that night I would outline it in my mind. A solution did not always come the next morning, but invariably some clarification resulted.

Although the idea was not new with Lindbergh, this approach to problem solving may help explain his surprising accomplishments as a medical researcher. During his work on the perfusion pump, for example, he was able to overcome at least one major difficulty that had appeared almost insurmountable to other scientists.

In the fifth dimension, Lindbergh was fascinated by the mystery of life, its meaning and quality in relation to its length. In his early laboratory work with Carrel at Rockefeller Institute, he toyed with the idea of extending physical life forever, picking up on his childhood question, why did people have to die? He wondered at Carrel keeping tissue from a chicken's heart alive in a flask for thirty-two years. Perhaps science could destroy death and keep the human heart going forever. Through his contribution to the perfusion pump, Lindbergh has indeed lengthened a vast number of lives. But keeping people alive soon receded as a genuine concern. He became less interested in quantity and more interested in quality. It was not so much the length of life that mattered, he believed. What you do with your time is more important than how much time you have.

Toward the close of his life, during his final visit to his Minnesota roots, Lindbergh said that civilization's progress can be measured only by the quality of life. "All the achievements of mankind," he concluded, "have value only to the extent that they preserve and improve the quality of life."

For himself, staying alive was never important. If life did not have adventure or quality, he saw no point to it. This outlook, of course, was an important source of his famous lack of fear. His approach was, "Give me liberty or give me death." When he first went into flying, people tried to discourage him by noting a pilot's short life expectancy. He responded:

> Of course I would like to become a centenarian, but I decided that ten years spent as the pilot of an airplane was in value worth more than an ordinary lifetime. I would rather live ten years of adventure than forty years of boredom.

On another occasion he said, "Any coward can criticize a pilot for running into a hill, but I would rather die on a mountainside than in bed." And when the New York doctors told him he had but a few days to live and urged him to stay with their sophisticated medical system, he said, "I would rather spend one day on Maui than thirty days in the hospital." (As it turned out he had not one, but eight satisfying days on Maui, after which he actually did die in bed.)

Lindbergh and his words are featured in the American Showcase at the Disney World Epcot Center in Orlando, Florida:

> What kind of man would live where there is no daring? I don't believe in taking foolish chances. But nothing can be accomplished without taking any chance at all.

Lindbergh revolutionized the twentieth century's concepts of time and space. Yet he was always looking beyond time and space.

5

Nerves of Steel

In the future, I decided, I would devote more attention to the core without renouncing civilization. The important thing was the core.

Not the least of Charles Lindbergh's notable attributes was his failure to crack under pressures to which no other man in modern times—or perhaps even in any times—has been subjected.

His daughter Reeve, speaking at a forum in Minneapolis in 1985, put it this way:

> I think what my father went through, the way he survived all the circumstances of his life and the way he came out, was just amazing. I can't believe he could do that. Strength was one of the most impressive things about him. He came right through the fire all his life. He was able to come out of it with a very strong philosophy, and a very strong sense of self—and without having been beaten down by some of the things that were hard for him. Some of these were the celebrity pressure, the kidnapping, the World War II experience. Those were some hard times. And he came out so strong, which was so terrific.

Much of his survival strategy was—just say no. Somehow or other, whether consciously or not, he came to the conclusion that saying no was the way to stay alive. He said no to just about everything, except

33

aviation, conservation, and family. Greta Garbo was not the only prominent Swede who wanted to be let alone.

When he made his famous flight, it was for him simply the next logical step in his chosen career—from barnstorming to the air corps, to airmail, to pushing aviation's limits, to capturing the Orteig Prize for the Atlantic Flight. After that, he planned to go back home and do whatever came next. When he landed in Paris, however, a basic conflict surfaced. The reaction of his machine to him, he understood—and was grateful. The reaction of the people to him, he did not understand—and was puzzled. He was both modest and innocent. When he arrived in Paris, he expected to be met by two or three French aviators who had heard about his attempt. They would help him store his plane in a hangar, he would talk briefly with a few reporters, then he would take a bus or taxi into town and find a hotel. Throughout his life he apparently believed that that was what should have happened. He was, of course, pleased that people were excited about aviation, since that was the point. But when the world exploded around him—not just as a successful pilot, but as a personality, a supercelebrity, a world hero—he regarded the hullabaloo as human folly. He said the point of the flight was twofold—his love of flying and his desire to develop aviation. But something else emerged after the fact, which no one anticipated and which he apparently never wished to understand. He was supplying something far beyond aviation. He was satisfying a profoundly important emotional need, more important for the public than for him. The resulting unexpected pressures on him as a person were overwhelming. And the only way he could figure to deal with the hero's status he had unwittingly and unwillingly achieved was to keep to his singleness of purpose. This he did, through all three areas where Reeve perceived his stamina—the celebrityhood, the kidnapping, and the prewar conflicts.

Statistics on the postflight bombardment of Lindbergh are mind boggling. Between May 21 and June 17, 1927, three and a half million letters, fourteen thousand parcels, five thousand containing gifts, and poems were delivered. One in five people sent a local press clipping about the flight. Correspondents sent $10,000 in return postage to insure a reply. Harold Bixby, namer and backer of the *Spirit of St. Louis,* acknowledged

200,000 letters of congratulations via printed postcard with the help of a crew from the Saint Louis Chamber of Commerce. More than fifteen thousand presents worth over $2 million, including a Gutenberg Bible, were received from sixty-nine countries. Most cities in the United States, and many overseas, struck off some kind of gold or silver medal or plaque. Lindbergh sent them all, along with the handwritten manuscript of his book, *We,* to the Missouri Historical Society, Forest Park, Saint Louis. Fitzhugh Green, the Naval writer whom Lindbergh asked to close *We* with a chronicle of the post-Flight events, estimated that newspapers used more than twenty-five thousand extra tons of newsprint in May and June 1927.

Frederick Lewis Allen wrote:

Wherever he went, crowds fought for a chance to be near him, medals were pinned on him, tributes were showered upon him, his coming and going was news. It was said that he could not even send his shirts to a laundry because they did not come back—they were too valuable as souvenirs. His picture hung in hundreds of school rooms and in thousands of homes. No living American—no dead American, save perhaps Abraham Lincoln—commanded such unswerving fealty. You might criticize Coolidge or Hoover or Ford or Edison or Bobby Jones or any other headline hero—but if you decried anything that Lindbergh did, you knew that you had wounded your auditors. For Lindbergh was a god. . . . Incredibly, he kept his head and his instinct for fine conduct.

Lindbergh was offered $500,000 to appear in one movie; $1 million to appear in another; $5 million for a motion picture contract; $1 million for a vaudeville agreement; $40,000 each to appear on twelve radio shows; $2.5 million to fly around the world; $240,000 to stand before a camera and read the first account of his flight. He was offered the presidency of a manufacturing company; a home in Flushing Meadows; $50,000 to endorse a cigarette, $100,000 to make a lecture tour. His total offers that summer reached at least $11 million, worth more than $90 million today.

Except for those related to aviation, he declined them all. "He was very upset," said Harry Bruno, a public relations man assigned to Lindbergh, "that people would offer him something for nothing." His response, in fact, was disconcertingly radical; if a celebrity of today turned down such megabucks, Donahue would call him un-American. Yet this unheard-of behavior may have saved him from being destroyed by Hollywood and Madison Avenue. It was also a major factor in his enormous popularity. Saying no made him all the more sought after. A friend has said that Lindbergh's place in history has been assured not only by what he did before and during his famous flight, but also by what he did not do after it. Professor Adams's comment was accurate: for the time, Lindbergh changed the reputation of human nature.

With all the glittering baubles that were danced before his eyes, how was it that this twenty-five-year-old airmail carrier could handle instant world statesmanship? From whence came the nerves of steel—beginning in the American Embassy in Paris and on out to the swirling pressures beyond? How could he have acted with such unerring grace, how come the sure-footed diplomacy? Much of this can be explained as but one of the innate gifts with which Lindbergh was endowed from conception. But Nancy Eubank, formerly of the Minnesota Historical Society, has offered an alternate insight. In 1985, she created an impressive photo display on Minnesota's famous son, set up beneath a replica of the *Spirit of St. Louis,* which still hangs in the Lindbergh terminal of the Minneapolis-Saint Paul airport. One of her captions noted that, engulfed by a maelstrom of unprecedented international and diplomatic attention, perhaps subconscious memories from his childhood in Washington came to his aid. With his Congressman father, he had learned how to meet eminent people. As a boy, for example, he had had a conversation with President Woodrow Wilson in the White House. "It was as if Lindbergh had been bred for this purpose," wrote biographer Walter Ross; like a young diplomat, he was "carefully tutored to meet royal occasions."

The frenzy that had begun to build before the takeoff from Long Island and had exploded worldwide upon the landing at Le Bourget became a roaring national conflagration back in America. The public passion for at least a glimpse of the daring and handsome hero was insatiable. He had wanted to fly the *Spirit of St. Louis* around Europe and Asia, the way he used to take his old Jenny around the American midwest. But the public's voracious appetite led President Calvin Coolidge to send the navy cruiser *USS Memphis* to Cherbourg with a request that Lindbergh immediately return to the United States. The pilot, in spite of all his Lone Eagle independence, took seriously his rank as captain in the Army Air Corps and treated the invitation as a directive from his commander-in-chief. On his first day back in America, he told about it to the National Press Club in Washington. His brief remarks, with uncharacteristic (in public) humor, were punctuated after each phrase, five times in all, by roars of laughter and applause:

> When I landed at Le Bourget a few weeks ago, I landed with the expectancy and the hope of being able to see Europe. . . . It was the first time I had ever been abroad . . . and I wasn't in any hurry to get back. . . . But I was informed that while it wasn't an order to come back home . . . that there'd be a battleship waiting for me—next week! . . .

He was no longer the free, fly-where-you-please-with-a-Rand-McNally-railroad-map, barnstorming spirit. All of a sudden, he was a prisoner of his fame.

Three weeks after Lindbergh landed in Paris, he was back in New York. On June 13, the city gave him the greatest tickertape parade in its long parade-jaded history. Two days later, he was the personal guest of Broadway showman Florenz Ziegfeld at the bright new theater bearing his name. The show that night happened to be the season's musical hit, *Rio Rita;* and for the pilot it was a kind of "make-up." He and his friends had been on their way to see that same play May 19, when they had to cancel to prepare for the Long Island takeoff the next morning.

Patricia Ziegfeld Stephenson, daughter of Florenz Ziegfeld and actress Billie Burke, was ten years old at the time. She has a vivid recollection of that night. Her father and Lindbergh sat in one row, she and her mother immediately behind. Patty saw none of the show. She spent all her time sliding down in her seat so that she could touch her foot against Lindbergh's. "Sit up, Patty," her mother admonished, "little girls don't do that." Whereupon she would slide down again. Mrs.

Stephenson still has the diminutive and elegant dress she wore that evening.

Mr. Ziegfeld, proud to be host to the hottest property he had ever booked, on stage or off, was anxious to introduce the superstar to his VIP friends. He invited them for intermission refreshments in his private quarters on a floor above. Soon after the lights came up, however, the honored guest vanished. At length the security people discovered he had locked himself in Mr. Ziegfeld's executive lavatory. The incident shows not only the pilot's penchant for escape, but his playfulness as well; he probably figured that leaving his host dangling in front of all those very important friends without the promised Hamlet was just the trick for the occasion.

Once Lindbergh had arrived back in America, the public clamor for at least a glimpse of the handsome young hero became overwhelming. Officials everywhere thought it would be a good thing for the people of the country to have an opportunity to see the man and his plane. Dwight Morrow told the Guggenheims, one of whose family foundations promoted aviation, that he believed it would also be a good thing for the pilot. It would give him a constructive task and help keep him ahead of the forces that might swallow him. Harry Guggenheim and Charles Lindbergh together decided on a three-month flying tour with the *Spirit of St. Louis*.

The Daniel Guggenheim Fund for the Promotion of Aeronautics financed the trip which was designed to allow at least one night in each of the forty-eight states. For public relations assistance, the Fund retained the best professional in the business. Still legendary today, Ivy Lee was known as a "physician to corporate bodies" and had been credited, among other things, with changing John D. Rockefeller's image from that of a ruthless oil baron to one of a philanthropist who handed out dimes. The rules sent out to each city stipulated that no admission would be charged for any event, there would be no commercial sponsorship anywhere along the line, and the pilot must be allowed to retire by nine o'clock each evening. The Department of Commerce, whose secretary was Herbert Hoover, provided an escort plane for support.

Before the odyssey could begin, however, Lindbergh had to satisfy a contractual obligation to Putnam, the publishing company, for a book about his flight. He thought the agreement was that he would be interviewed by a professional writer, who would then narrate the account in the third person. When the pilot discovered that the professional was to write it in the first person, he declined. "I didn't want a ghostwritten book to come out over my name," he said. With less than a month before his tour was to begin, Harry and Carol Guggenheim invited him to stay with them at their Long Island home Falaise, a Norman-style mansion of thirty rooms on Sands Point with its own private landing strip. There in June and July the twenty-five-year old college dropout cranked forth forty-five thousand words in three weeks, in longhand on legal-size yellow sheets. He was protected by the servants and the estate's security system. While the world was going crazy outside, the pilot remained in seclusion for twenty-four days—broken only once by a three-day ceremonial trip to Ottawa, honoring Canada's sixtieth anniversary. The book, entitled *We*, was rushed to the public in July, and by the end of August it had already been reprinted a dozen times. It became a bestseller for two years and was the beginning of still another distinguished career: Lindbergh as an author. He would be writing on carbon-paper pads on his lap in odd corners of the earth for the rest of his life and would produce seven books, one of them a Pulitzer Prize winner.

The forty-eight-state tour began July 20 at Mitchel Field, Long Island, and ended there October 23, taking a counterclockwise course to the north, across to the west, south, and back east. Lindbergh was mobbed everywhere, and his nervous strength was incredible.

Donald E. Keyhoe, pilot and writer, with an assignment from *National Geographic,* was assigned by the Commerce Department to coordinate details of the tour. Lindbergh requested that Phil Love, his old buddy from army and airmail days, pilot the escort plane. The three handled the pressure by having a rollicking time. To read Keyhoe's book *Flying With Lindbergh* is to play along with three wisecracking, practical-joking characters having a ball behind closed doors—even fishing in the wilderness—between public appearances. The stern, cool image of the young celebrity belied the prankster kid underneath. One evening, for example, after the hero had made his standard speech for aviation at one of the eighty-two civic banquets he addressed that summer and fall, the three returned to their quarters, and while Love took a shower, Lindbergh doused him with a pitcher of ice water, having arranged with Keyhoe to slam the door behind him as he fled ahead of the irate Love. Should one of them be late turning in, he might find his sheets sewn up. Once when Keyhoe was opening his camera, a fish fell out of the lens. Some measure of equilibrium was no doubt maintained by letting the small boy out of the adult shell.

Lindbergh also found that escaping to the wilderness, always his friend, helped relieve some of the pressure. In early September, about half-way through the tour, he took more than six hours to cover the sixty-five-mile distance between Butte and Helena. He detoured, he wrote in *Autobiography of Values,* "over lakes and forests, over Glacier National Park, even crossing the Canadian border . . . just to have time to think without distraction."

The Tour, like the Flight, was an impressive feat of endurance. In August, Will Rogers wrote, "I saw a late picture of Lindbergh, that banquet chicken is slowly getting him." By early October, the city-hopping hero must have been glad it was about over. A press photo of the parade in Memphis, with still three weeks to go on the tour, shows tickertape streaming from the upper reaches of the downtown canyon and the business-suited hero in the center. No dignitary sits with him in the open-top back seat; he is all alone at the bottom of a huge urban funnel, neither smiling nor waving, the youthful honoree, lost in his own reflections, impassive, impersonal, holding to what he later called his "core."

To escape from the celebrity pressures, Lindbergh, like a buck during the northern Minnesota deer season, learned how to stay out of the way, take advantage of protective coloring, and bound into brush cover. It is impossible for anyone who is not Charles Lindbergh to appreciate the pressure on his nerves to which he was subjected—or to which he permitted himself to be subjected. Jim Newton tells of sitting with Charles on a bank in the remote Florida Everglades. Waiting for the tide and supplies, they thought they were secure in the wilderness. All of a sudden a small party in a boat came by out of nowhere. One of them said, "There he is!" Charles's face went white—he had been discovered. How many hundreds of times can a nervous system stand that kind of blanching? In India he experimented with controlling his pulse. Did he learn how to control nerve shock?

In 1934, Charles and Anne were in southern California visiting her sister Elisabeth, who was seriously ill. Will and Betty Rogers, away on a world tour, had turned over their Santa Monica Canyon ranch to the couple to use during their stay. The Lindberghs had been there only four days when they received a telephone call from the chief of the New Jersey State Police, Col. Norman Schwarzkopf. (His son was to lead the allied forces in the 1991 Persian Gulf War.) Bruno Hauptmann had been apprehended in New York as a kidnap suspect, and Lindbergh's testimony was needed at the extradition proceedings.

On March 1, 1932, the Lindberghs' first-born, twenty-month-old Charles Augustus Lindbergh Jr., had been stolen from a second-floor bedroom at their new home in Hopewell, New Jersey. The hair-raising ransom negotiations, sensationalized by the yellow press, turned out to be spurious when the baby's body, probably dead from a fractured skull in a ladder accident the night of the kidnapping, was found in a shallow roadside grave not far away.

The thirty-one-day prosecution of Bruno Hauptmann for murder in the Flemington, New Jersey, courthouse was called "the trial of the century" by Hearst reporter Adela Rogers St. Johns. There had never been anything like it, and, because of the subsequent correction of its abuses, there probably will not be again. From the outset, the trial took on the trappings of a circus. One eye-witness called it "an obscene spectacle." The elements that converged on the tiny courthouse made for big news—supercelebrity parents grieving for their murdered baby, money changing hands through mysterious go-betweens. Again the attention of the world focused on this one man. Whereas he had hoped that his pursuit of a normal life would quiet the public's interest in him, it was now fanned to new intensity. Newspaper circulation went up some twenty percent in the three weeks after the kidnapping. When the trial came along, three hundred reporters descended on the village, including the brightest names in journalism: Walter Winchell, Edna Ferber, Fanny Hurst, Damon Runyon, Kathleen Norris, and Alexander Wolcott. William Randolph Hearst sent not only St. Johns, but also his front-page political "think" columnist, Arthur Brisbane. During the first two weeks of the trial, nine million words poured out in the daily accounts. Outside the courthouse, the telegraph wires from the press room were so thick that they appeared black against the sky, and when traversing the pole, they made a gigantic cross, which one writer saw as symbolic of the crucifixion of Charles and Anne Lindbergh. In addition, hundreds of thousands of persons were attracted to Flemington. Many waited in line to get in—sometimes in sleet, rain, and cold. There was only one hotel and one bar in the entire town.

Press hysteria mounted. While the case was on the front pages, the couple received 100,000 letters a day. On other occasions, Lindbergh usually wore various disguises to protect himself from the public, but during the trial he came as he was. In spite of his abhorrence of public appearances, he arrived every day the court was in session during the six weeks from January 3 to February 13, even on the days he was not required on the witness stand. Adela Rogers St. Johns wondered "how he could have sat there for thirty-one days and never had to be restrained from trying to get his hands on Hauptmann four chairs away." On the first day that Anne took the stand, she recounted every agonizing detail of the life of her baby, particularly the last day before he was stolen. She spoke for forty-three minutes. Later she wrote, "I feel as if it were a poison working in my system, this idea of the crime. How deep will it eat into our lives?"

Fifty years later, when Mrs. Hauptmann, still convinced of her husband's innocence, persuaded New Jersey officials to review the case, Mrs. Lindbergh was asked her reactions. "If they open up that matter," she said, "we would have to go over all that evidence, and I just don't think I could go through it again." The state attorney general's office, after studying twenty thousand documents, concluded that justice had been done and again closed the case.

Although the Lindberghs would go into voluntary exile in England later that year to escape the pressure, the nervous strength of the Lone Eagle throughout the ordeal was extraordinary.

Lindbergh's nerves of steel in the months before America's entry into World War II—a period of family torment vividly described in Anne's book *War Within and Without*—will be explored in Chapter 16.

6

The Personal Person

I'll be honest with you. I never once thought I would not make it.

In spite of the fact that he had the world at his feet, that he could have had almost anything he wanted, Lindbergh remained a considerate and caring person. These traits appeared early in his relationship with his parents. Although his mother and father drifted apart when he was very young, causing him a little boy's pain and sadness, he maintained a close, loving companionship with each of them, and they with him. Affection was expressed the Swedish way, by handshakes rather than hugs. The best-pal stories of father and son—hunting, swimming, and canoeing in the wooded waterways of Minnesota—sound truly idyllic. C.A. died three years before his son's Flight, but Evangeline was there for both the preparation for take-off and the storm of welcome home. When the *USS Memphis* arrived back from France in June 1927 with the crated *Spirit of St. Louis* safely stowed in the hold, the first person Lindbergh saw was his mother. The gangplank came down at the Navy dockyard in the Potomac River, and Vice Admiral Guy H. Burrage, commanding officer of the voyage, went ashore to return shortly with Evangeline Lindbergh on his arm. Then, for almost an hour, the excited nation had to wait—press, radio, public officials, and the president of the United States—while mother and son had their own private rendezvous in a cabin aboard.

The following year, Lindbergh decided it was time to think about a family of his own and started getting serious about finding the right girl to marry. He had no dating history. He was so shy in his younger days that he would cross over to the other side when he saw a girl coming toward him on the street. Two-some socializing was even less possible as he became more famous. To facilitate his search process, Lindbergh drew up scientific qualifications for his love, as though he were listing desirable attributes in livestock for his old farm. He spoke of the "overwhelming importance of genes and chromosomes . . . good health, good form, good sight and hearing. Such qualities could be outlined in sequence like the specifications for an airplane." He wanted to marry a girl who liked flying, because he would take her with him on expeditions.

There is a curious stipulation in his checklist: "I took for granted, too, that I would marry a girl who had no strong ties to any church, because I believed freedom of thought would be essential in my home." In other words in *his* home there would be freedom of thought about every subject except one. On that one, he would decide in advance how it would be. Hang your clothes in the freedom tree, but don't go near the church water.

In thinking over the women he had encountered, Charles experienced a flashback to the Morrow family. He had met the four children of Ambassador and Mrs. Morrow when he visited Mexico City in 1927, following the forty-eight-state tour. Their second daughter, Anne, now came up on his mental screen. Because she had not made much impression on his conscious mind earlier, he was surprised to find her conspicuous in memory months after he left Mexico City. Anne says he noticed her because when she sat next to him at dinner, she was quiet and did not, like the others, try to make conversation. It is possible, of course, that she was showing a keen instinct for the exact manner required to attract this particular man.

Charles insisted he would marry someone he loved, regardless of other factors, although he had also said one could fall in love with the "right" person after that person had been determined. Obviously Anne met the love requirement. As to the other qualifications, the genes seemed to be satisfactory, coming from such a distinguished family. She had good health, excellent eyesight and good hearing, and a rather slight form, but one that turned out to be capable of bearing six healthy children. She forced herself to like flying, and then really did. As to the religious test, her family were faithful members of the First Presbyterian Church of Englewood, New Jersey, and she was agreeable to the tradition. Her father was on the Board of Union Theological Seminary in New York; a member of its faculty, William Adams Brown, conducted Charles and Anne's wedding ceremony. It is not known what Charles's definition was of "strong ties to any church," nor is it clear how committed she would have to have been in order to fail the ecclesiastical criterion. Apparently on this score as on the others, she was clean, or at least clean enough. Anne's writings are filled with allusions to the Bible, of which she shows an extraordinary knowledge and understanding. If she did have strong ties to a church, she managed to keep them under good control. In spite of achieving world fame herself as an independent personality, she was in many ways a dutiful and submissive wife, one that would follow her husband's lead. After Charles died and before Anne left Hawaii, she regularly attended the Congregational Church in Hana, Maui. Following the service she usually made some perceptive comment to the minister about the sermon. She continued to carry the small New Testament that was the only book Charles took with him to the South Pacific in World War II.

On their first date, in 1928, Charles took Anne up in a plane over Long Island. On the second, during a ride over New Jersey roads in his Franklin air-cooled auto, they were engaged. On Sunday, May 27, 1929, they were married. It was a typical secretive operation. The pilot's mother was just back from a teaching stint at the American College in Istanbul, and Anne's parents invited a few guests to meet her at a reception. The Morrows were always having occasions at their home in Englewood, and the coming and going this weekend made no special impression in the news-gatherers' vigil outside the gate. Around noon, the principals turned up in the living room in appropriate dress, Dr. Brown stepped forth, and the deed was done. The couple cut the wedding cake, sipped ginger ale, changed back into the clothes they wore upon entering the gates earlier, and were driven out. It was hours before the press learned what had happened.

The honeymoon was by private boat from Long Island up to Maine. They managed to elude the news people for ten days. But when they stopped at a Maine port for supplies, a number of press boats pursued and circled the couple for six hours. Photographers threw bottles at the honeymoon craft, hoping for a picturable response. They got none.

In all, the Lindberghs had six children, five of them still living—Charles Augustus (1930–1932); Jon Morrow (b. 1932), a deep-sea diver and marine agriculturalist who lives near Seattle; Land Morrow (b. 1937), a Montana cattle rancher; Anne Spencer (b. 1940), a writer of children's books who lives in Vermont; Scott Morrow (b. 1942), a researcher in Brazil on primates and endangered species; and Reeve Morrow (b. 1945), also a writer and an executive of the Charles A. Lindbergh Fund. She, too, lives in Vermont. Reeve writes and speaks in public with great pride in her father. She even gives autographs. The others are more private, like their father preferring to be neither heard nor seen, but willing to surface on occasion for an interview or quotation.

They grew up in Darien, Connecticut. Furniture in the house was simple, but hardly Spartan, coming mostly from the Morrow household and much of it quite valuable furnishings from Europe. To his children, Lindbergh was always "Father." He had many principles, theories, and standards. He never forgot the words his own father spoke to him as a child, "A boy is a boy; two boys are half a boy; three boys are no boy at all." The more people that are involved, the less gets done. It was the Lone Eagle again. He wrote in *The Spirit of St. Louis* about his takeoff from Roosevelt Field:

> By flying alone, above all, I've gained in freedom. I haven't had to keep a crew member acquainted with my plans. My movements weren't restricted by someone else's temperament, health, or knowledge. My decisions aren't weighted by responsibility for another's life . . . When I was sitting in my cockpit on the muddy runway, in the tail wind, there was no one to warp my judgment with a "Hell, let's try it!" or "It looks pretty bad to me." I've not been enmeshed in petty quarreling and heavy organizational problems. Now I can go on or turn

back according to the unhampered dictates of my mind and senses. According to that saying of my father's, I'm a full boy—independent—alone.

Particularly with his sons, Lindbergh stressed this attitude of non-protective self-reliance. Will Rogers, the last journalist to see the Lindberghs' baby Charles, two weeks before the kidnapping, gives us this glimpse:

> His dad was pitching a soft sofa pillow at him as he was tod-
> dling around. The weight of it would knock him over. I asked
> Lindy if he was rehearsing him for forced landings. After about
> the fourth time of being knocked over he did the cutest thing.
> He dropped of his own accord when he saw it coming.

As in many families, there were some sharp conflicts between father and sons, most acutely with his youngest son, Scott. A major issue between them was the Vietnam War. Lindbergh, an active consultant to the Pentagon, thought American war policy was not well designed, but, as in World War II, believed a citizen must support his government once the war is started. Some of his offspring, who were children of the 1960s, were strongly opposed. Lively family discussions ensued. The division with Scott was the most intense, and this and other problems led to years of unhappiness between them. The relationship was finally healed, however, in conversations between the two during Lindbergh's last days on Maui. Helpful talks also took place that week between Scott's older brother Jon and his father.

Over and beyond his approach to family life, Lindbergh's moral discipline, one of the reasons for his immense popularity in the twenties, is notable partly because it came out of no particular religious impulses, but rather seems to have welled up out of his own essence, and the unusual influences of his heredity and environment. Anne writes that in the Mexico City days her father was pointing out Lindbergh to his daughters as a fine young man who did not smoke or drink or run around.

The particulars of Lindbergh's character also included scrupulous honesty, a quality central to his rigorous personal code. He could not countenance a book purporting to be written by him if, in fact, it was written by someone else. Even the assumed names he used while travelling were variations of his own, such as "Charles August." Betty Gow, the young Scots nurse who looked after the Lindbergh baby at the fateful home in Hopewell, New Jersey, told a fellow passenger on a ship back to Britain:

> Colonel Lindbergh is the most honest man I have ever met. He cannot tell a lie even if he knows the truth is going to hurt. He just has to tell the truth, and he expects other people to tell the truth to him.

There was an earlier young American who said, "I cannot tell a lie." His name came up in a conversation at an embassy reception during the Vietnam War, which Lindbergh supported, on the subject of defoliation, which he did not. One of the guests recalls Lindbergh saying:

> Once upon a time I thought George Washington was a good hero for American children, because when he cut down the cherry tree, he admitted it later on. Now I'd have the story omitted from the American history books. Even owning up doesn't excuse cutting down a tree.

He supported the honesty all right; he just did not like continuing the spotlight on the sin that needed confessing. Truth was central to Lindbergh's sense of values:

> I've learned not to trust people who are inaccurate. Every aviator knows that if mechanics are inaccurate, aircraft crash. If pilots are inaccurate, they get lost—sometimes killed. In my profession, life itself depends on accuracy.

Each year at income tax time, after figuring what he owed the government, he made out his check for an additional ten percent. For him, it was a combination of honesty, just to be sure, and patriotism, an immigrant son's gratitude. The practice stood him in good stead when the White House declared war on him and called for a check of his tax records. He told them to go ahead and look.

Other stories are told about the human Lindbergh. In the winter of 1928, when he was working on a combination air-rail plan for transporting passengers across the country, he periodically visited the family of William W. Atterbury, president of the Pennsylvania Railroad, at their home on Philadelphia's Main Line. Two of Atterbury's sons were pilots, and around a Sunday dinner table they asked their guest what it was like flying across the Atlantic. His reply:

> I think the only way I can tell you is this. Why don't you get up at twelve o'clock tonight, go into the bathroom, turn the light off, open the window and get it as cold as you can, get two or three alarm clocks (for dials), have a little flashlight. You can't see anything. Every once in a while you use the flashlight to see one of the dials on the board. And you kind of wish you weren't so far from home. You just persevere. You say, I will do what the compass says. I will stay that way. I know what my altitude is. And I know I'll make it. I'll be honest with you, and I don't want to sound conceited, but I never once thought I would not make it.

When Minnesota Governor Elmer L. Andersen was enlisting Lindbergh's aid in persuading authorities to establish Voyageurs National Park in the Rainy River area on the Canadian border, the flyer asked to see the site. Andersen and Minnesota historian Russell Fridley arranged to take him there. They would need a plane, so they telephoned the manager of the International Falls Airport to rent one. Lindbergh was at their side during the call.

"Do you have a pilot?" the manager asked.

"Yes, we have a pilot."

"What kind of plane can he fly?"

Lindbergh got out his wallet and showed some of his licenses. Elmer began to read them off over the phone. He came to one that was all-purpose, all-nation.

"Oh, hell," the manager broke in, "if he's got that, he can fly anything."

Practical jokester Charles appreciated the airport manager's chagrin when the party arrived with their "pilot."*

Lindbergh was constantly on the go, and before he departed from the Pan American office in New York, he would stop for a friendly word with the woman who arranged his tickets. One time she told him about her new apple trees and an expensive gadget she and her husband were thinking of acquiring for fertilizing them. When the traveler returned two weeks later, he called her and said he had figured out a simpler, cheaper way to care for her saplings. Somehow, during a trip that probably resulted in significant recommendations to Pan Am and the U.S. Air Force, he took time to think of a woman in the office and her apple trees.

I myself experienced something of the Lindbergh modesty. He had heard that I had had some success in arranging with the Immigration and Naturalization Service for the entry into the U.S. of two dozen Moral Re-Armament personnel who had been hung up on various borders. He had been frustrated in trying to gain admission for a number of Romanians in whom he was interested, and when we were visiting at the Shoreham Hotel in Washington, he asked how I did it. He seemed to pick up on an idea I gave him, but I never heard what happened to the Roman-

---

*Incidents like this had a way of happening. When Lindbergh wanted to rent a Stinson 90 in Colorado Springs to give an overview of the surrounding terrain to two colleagues on the Air Force Academy Site Selection Committee, the airport manager did not recognize him and asked, "Do you know how to fly?"

"I think I can fly."

"Do you have a license?"

"Yes, I have a license."

"Well," said the manager, "If you will come into my office, I'll look over your papers."

At his desk in the little room with its broken-down furniture and cracked walls, the manager said, "Let's see your license." The aviator of course had about a dozen from all over the world, each bearing his photograph. As the man looked at them and then up at his visitor, his face reddened.

"You ain't Charles Lindbergh, are you?" he stammered.

"Yes, I am."

"My God!"

ians. I do recall his expressing the wish that he not do anything that would interfere with the MRA program.

Michael Collins had a similar experience. He was the astronaut who orbited the moon while Neil Armstrong and Edwin "Buzz" Aldrin walked on the surface. He invited Lindbergh to write the foreword to his book, *Carrying the Fire*. Here is Collins's reaction:

> The two qualities I was most struck with were the thoughtfulness and the humility of the man. He was doing me an extraordinary favor, one that required long and uncompensated hours of his time. Yet he acted as if our roles were reversed, as if I were bestowing some honor on him.

For a man who had an image of austerity, there was in his interpersonal relationships an unusual sensitivity.

7

The Cowboy and the Pilot

You know that kid has quite a bit of determination. I have noticed little things about him that shows that he has a will of his own.   Will Rogers

The momentous fame of Will Rogers and Charles Lindbergh, the two greatest heroes of the twentieth century, was all the more remarkable because the stature of neither hung on political or military achievements, the usual roads to the history books. Rogers, particularly at first, did much to humanize the young pilot in the public mind. Although Lindbergh had that winning smile, he often came off as a fairly severe, humorless young man. Rogers, in his folksy way, was able to get beneath that facade, and give millions of people a different look.

With his rope tricks, chewing gum, and cracks about politicians and current events, Rogers had been the star of the Ziegfeld Follies on Broadway for years. By the time Lindbergh burst on the scene, he had moved west, and would soon become Hollywood's top box-office attraction. Rogers's greatest impact on the public, and the factor that gave him enormous clout in Washington and everywhere else, came through his universally read, telegram-length, daily column, which appeared in 400 newspapers and reached some forty million people, or about one third of the nation.

There was a twenty-three-year age difference between the two, Rogers having been born in 1879, Lindbergh in 1902. They were notably similar in background. Both grew up outdoors—Rogers in the grasslands of eastern Oklahoma, Lindbergh in the forests of central Minnesota—which gave to each an unusual appreciation of nature and its life cycles, an ingredient that minimized their concern about physical survival, and gave them both a lack of fear. Their attitudes toward death were similar—you do what you think you should do, and let the consequences take care of themselves. Both had successful fathers, financially and politically. Clem Rogers was a prosperous rancher who helped write the Oklahoma constitution; C. A. Lindbergh was a prominent attorney, land developer, and U.S. congressman. The two heroes were known for their exemplary personal and family lives. Both were blessed with powerful physiques that glowed with health, and their captivating grins gave them an all-American look that gathered everyone in.

The greatest dissimilarity was in their attitudes toward the press and public. The one mastered every means of public communication and joined a crowd like a man entering a warm bath. The other hated every minute of it.

In May 1927, Will Rogers joined the rest of the human race in enthusiasm for the daring young man in his flying machine. In his daily column of May 20, the humorist wrote he would make no attempt at jokes because everyone was praying for Lindbergh. The day after the successful landing in Paris, Will thought the greatest thing the feat demonstrated was that "a person could still get the entire front pages without murdering anybody." Two days later, he hoped the young pilot would be allowed some freedom.

> There is a hundred and twenty million people in America all ready to tell Lindbergh what to do. The first thing we want to get into our heads is that this boy is not our usual type of hero that we are used to dealing with. He is all the others rolled into one and then multiplied by ten, and his case must be treated in a more dignified way . . . Let him have his entire time open to assist aviation, then he will be a blessing to us and not a side show . . . I will personally play benefits for him the rest of my

life to keep him from having to make exhibitions out of himself. We only get one of these in a lifetime.

> Yours, one of the hundred million advisers, Will Rogers

Two weeks after the Flight, he was still trying to explain the Lindbergh
phenomenon:

> The more you read of him and his actions, and the way he has
> conducted himself in Paris and the rest of the country has been
> a great satisfaction to all of us. The ones of us here now will
> never live to see a thing that will give us a bigger kick than his
> flight did. It was the greatest wished-for and prayed-for
> achievement that ever happened or ever will happen in our life-
> time. Prayers was what he was sailing on. And what a smart
> fellow he turned out to be in everything that he did after he got
> there! Why, we never had a diplomat that conducted himself
> with as fitting grace as this lad did.

. . . as well as what the new hero might do for all aspects of aviation:

> Now, if we can keep him out of show business and the movies.
> . . . He is at the top of a profession that is just starting to get
> somewhere. He might be the means of saving us in the next
> war.

Rogers suggested boycotting any newspaper that used the word "Lucky"
in connection with Lindbergh. He thought it was a polite way of "lessen-
ing the glory of his feat." But on one of his weekly radio broadcasts in
1930, he said, "He ain't lucky. Yes, I'll take that back, he is lucky—I
met his wife."

The companionship of the two heroes was a natural. Rogers was at
the time the most influential nonpilot promoter of aviation, both commercial and military. Their friendship was probably more extensive than
we know, but we have a few peeks. They hit it off right away at their
first meeting in San Diego during the forty-eight-state welcome-home
tour. In his column of September 20, 1927, Rogers wrote:

> Leaving tonight to go to make a speech at Lindbergh's banquet.
> It wouldn't be so hard to speak if you knew anything of impor-
> tance he had ever done.

At the San Diego dinner, held in the historic Hotel Del Coronado, superlatives rolled on about the young pilot and his records. When Rogers's turn came, he said:

> Colonel, all these records of yours will be broken. The planes will be bigger and faster. But these other orators ain't mentioned the one record that will remain unsurpassed and go down through the ages. This is that you are the only man who ever took a ham sandwich to Paris.

The next day Lindbergh parked the *Spirit of St. Louis* and flew a dozen VIP's, including Will and Betty Rogers, from San Diego to Los Angeles in a Ford Tri-Motor. Will reported on one of his Sunday evening radio broadcasts:

> We was going to land in a field near Inglewood (later to become Los Angeles International Airport), and there wasn't no sock blowing to show which way the wind was blowing. I was sitting in the seat by him, and I said, "Colonel, how can you tell how to land when you can't tell what way the wind is blowing?" He said, "Didn't you see the way those clothes were blowing on the line back there a while ago?" So I said, "Well what would you do if it wasn't Monday?" To show you this guy has a good sense of humor, he come right back at me and said, "I wouldn't fly over such a dirty place."

That afternoon at a reception in the Ambassador Hotel, Lindbergh was besieged for his autograph by movie stars accustomed to giving other people their autographs. Mary Pickford tried without success to get them to ease off. Will wrote:

> DeMille had him autograph each of his commandments. Sam Goldwyn had him sign a paper that if he ever married, he would be allowed to stage the wedding. Louis B. Mayer wanted him to autograph the MGM lion. Tom Mix had him autograph a hat. I bet Lindy cursed the day he learned to write.

The next time the two celebrities met was later that year, December 1927, when Dwight W. Morrow, U.S. ambassador to Mexico, invited them both to Mexico City in an effort to improve the relationship between the two countries.

It was on this occasion that the aviator met his future wife, the ambassador's daughter Anne. Rogers was as impressed with the diplomatic sensitivity the young pilot showed in Mexico as he had been with Lindbergh's conduct in Paris. Charles invited Will to go up with him in a rickety old local plane, but said, "I won't take you up first. It wouldn't look good to come to Mexico and take up an American first." In his column Rogers wrote, "Morrow and I have resigned as ambassadors in Mexico. Now there is only one when he is in the country." Lindbergh steadfastly resisted personal questions, feeling the answers were nobody's business but his own. But Rogers, a great communicator, understood the things people were interested in, and described what he observed, "If you have wondered what a hero eats for breakfast, he had fruit, ham and eggs and toast and coffee, just about what a common feller will eat when he can get it."

Will noticed the importance Charles attached to punctuality. "Lindbergh, the best ambassador in the world, is never late. If he says I will arrive in Siberia at 3:30, at 3:29 he will be there." A Midwest college professor echoed the observation, "These other pilots land late, or in the water, or in another country, but Lindbergh always does what he says he is going to do."

The lives of Lindbergh and Rogers intersected at playful times and sad times. Charles had declined Will's invitation to attend the opening of the new Ziegfeld Follies Extravaganza in the fall of 1928, but called Will at the last minute to say he had just broken free, and asked if he could still come. The humorist scrambled to come up with tickets and switched Carl Fisher, the Indianapolis Speedway founder and Miami Beach developer, to other seats.

Rogers was famous for his on-stage kidding of the celebrities who frequented his shows. He once roped Thomas Edison while the inventor was dozing in his seat. Lindbergh knew that he would present a temptation to the entertainer and said, "Don't you start any of your funny business on me," adding that this went for the theater management and spotlight people too. Will reassured him. It was an excruciating predicament for the humorist. He always introduced the notables present, and here was the world's most famous celebrity, for whom he was loaded with a pocketful of gags about funny things the two had done in Mexico. But he held back and said not one word about Lindbergh, who in gratitude came back to the dressing room reporting that he had won a twenty dollar bet that Will would not make him bow or something. "I told him I was a bigger hero than he was," Rogers wrote, "that it took more nerve for me NOT to talk about him than he showed flying the ocean."

When Will and Betty invited Charles and Anne to use their ranch in the Santa Monica Canyon during their visit to Anne's sister Elisabeth in Pasadena, the only member of the Rogers clan around was son Jim, who came back ahead of the family to return to Pomona College. One morning at breakfast, Jim watched with some dismay Charles putting honey on his Mexican beans, and protested that it was a fine way to ruin good beans. "Don't knock it if you haven't tried it," said Charles in effect, and made Jim a convert. When the Lindberghs were called east on account of the Hauptmann case, Jim and ranch steward Emil Sandmeier, spirited the couple down a dirt trail used by the Rogers's polo ponies and made an end run around the reporters waiting at the gate.

A year later Will Rogers died in a plane crash in Alaska. Charles immediately telephoned Betty, offering to send a Pan American plane to bring home the bodies of her husband and Wiley Post, the pilot. She gratefully accepted. Thus ended a chapter in the relationship of two giants of their time—Charles Lindbergh and Will Rogers—so similar and yet so different, key players in defining the twentieth century.

8

Germany and the Fall From Grace

Show me a hero and I will write you a tragedy.
F. Scott Fitzgerald

Will Rogers put it this way, "One day you are a Senator, and the next you are paying for your postage stamps." Seldom has any one plummeted so quickly from god to bum as Charles Lindbergh did in the two years between 1939 and 1941.

The descent was not due to his opposing America's drift toward war. At the time he was speaking for America's heartland. The polls then indicated that fully eighty percent of the people agreed with him. Rather his problems came out of a combination of a widespread misunderstanding of his prewar activities in Germany and, in a measure, of his own insensitivity. It was a particularly difficult time for both husband and wife. Anne was loyal to Charles and his non-interventionist convictions throughout, but her family, a dedicated component of what was called the "eastern establishment" and active in the committees supporting Great Britain, was highly critical of the couple's position. She felt more insulated than her husband, because he at least had some solace in the memory of his father's opposition to World War I. "We are alone," she said, "and probably always will be from now on."

Even his old home town backed away. Ever since the Flight, the high water tower that dominated the local skyline had proudly proclaimed that Little Falls was the boyhood home of a world hero. Now the large letters were painted out. Trans World Airlines (TWA), successor company to the Lindbergh-generated Transcontinental Air Transport (TAT), had from the beginning, carried on their fuselages a noble emblem: THE LINDBERGH LINE. The connection was now an economic liability, and the magic name was removed. Movements that would have been pleased with even a tenuous association with the aviator were now fearful he might appear favorable.

The change in the public's perception of Lindbergh was related in several ways to his character and philosophy and was caused by a complex convolution of aviation activities abroad and hard-ball politics at home.

On October 18, 1938, Field Marshal Hermann Goering, builder of the German Luftwaffe and his country's chief economic officer, presented Charles A. Lindbergh with a high civilian medal, the *Verdienstkreuz der Deutscher Adler,* the Service Cross of the German Eagle. The occasion was a dinner given by American Ambassador Hugh R. Wilson at the U.S. Embassy in Berlin. It was a stag affair, and Anne Lindbergh did not attend. Later that evening, however, when her husband showed her the medal, with uncanny foreboding she at once exclaimed, "The albatross." Even now, the award is for Charles Lindbergh an albatross. Today when asked who Lindbergh was, people are apt to say he flew the Atlantic, his baby was kidnapped, and he was decorated by the Nazis.

Here is the background. Ambassador Wilson was anxious to talk to Goering at an intimate, off-the-record dinner. The year before, the Field Marshal had succeeded Hjalmar Schacht as economic dictator of Germany, and Wilson hoped he could persuade Goering to allow emigrating Jews to take property out of the country with them. Up to that time they were permitted to leave, but they had to leave penniless, making for hardship on both the individuals themselves and the communities to which they immigrated. Wilson, who needed some kind of bait to help insure Goering's acceptance, invited Col. Lindbergh, who was in the country at the time, to attend also. The strategy worked. Goering was an aviator out of the old seat-of-the-pants, open-cockpit days, and like all pilots everywhere, was an admiring Lindbergh fan. The medal itself, which became such an impediment to the American, was awarded for "services to world aviation, and particularly for the historic 1927 solo flight across the Atlantic." Lindbergh had received thousands of similar medallions from cities and nations around the world, all of which he shipped by the bushel to the Missouri Historical Society. He treated this one like all the rest.

The gesture was unexpected by both the recipient and the embassy officials. There was no opportunity for seasoned foreign service officers to anticipate a potentially dangerous scene and prepare a diplomatic solution. Late in the day of the dinner—when no American official was still on duty—the German Air Ministry telephoned a message to an embassy clerk, a communmication that was not seen on any desk until the next morning. When Lindbergh arrived for the occasion, he and the others were surprised to see Goering approach him before dinner, begin speaking to him in German, which he did not understand, and hand him a red box. The recipient flashed his famous smile, and expressed his appreciation. He was not unaccustomed to receiving boxes with medals in them.

Lindbergh's conduct at the time, and his subsequent attitude, give us another look at the character and philosophy of the man. To begin with, the diplomatic sensitivity of the dinner's purpose forbade explanation to the public. Confidentiality was essential to the proposal for helping the Jews. Furthermore, if Lindbergh had declined the award, after having accepted undifferentiated thousands of others, it would have been a double affront—an insult to the special guest, the field marshal, and an insult to the host, the American ambassador. Three years later Wilson wrote to Lindbergh:

> Neither you nor I nor any other American present had a previous hint that the presentation would be made. I have always felt that if you had refused the decoration, presented under these circumstances, you would have been guilty of a breach of good taste. It would have been an act offensive to the guest of the Ambassador of your country, in the house of the Ambassador.

Critics who are prepared to accept this reasoning, argue that he should have later *returned* the medal. Three weeks after that critical dinner would have been a good time, when the first national, government-sponsored pogrom broke. Lindbergh was indeed so outraged by the horrors of the anti-Jewish persecution that he left the country in protest. But it would be surprising if he would have thought about the medal, probably already on its way back to Saint Louis. The next logical time he could have returned the decoration would have been in December 1941, when Hitler declared war on the United States, and the pilot himself plunged into the effort to defeat the Axis powers. He could have said then that the medal now represented an enemy state, and hence, it was no longer appropriate for him to keep it. Then, too, while still leaving the medal in Saint Louis, he might have made a simple statement of disavowal.

Lindbergh did not do any of this. It would have been unusual if he had. "Let bygones be bygones" was his way. Just as he resisted being flown again to Paris by drawing-room conversationalists, so he saw no point in rehashing an old Berlin dinner party. He considered that on the 1938 occasion, which took place while he was on a military and diplomatic mission, he had as a good soldier carried out what he was asked to do. He believed he had done the right thing for his country at the time. Subsequent events did not change that moment. If there were public relations consequences, it was no concern of his. He never endorsed anything in his life except the brand of gasoline that took him to Paris. If some people wished to twist his acceptance of a medal into some kind of approval of the medal's grantor, that was *their* problem. "Never complain, never explain."

Did he have later thoughts? Lone Eagles who conquer the world do not rush to suggest they might have done something differently. In 1955 Lindbergh wrote to his friend Truman Smith:

> The decoration Goering gave me that night never caused me any worry, and I doubt it caused much additional difficulty. It turned out to be a convenient object of attack for our political opposition; but if there had been no decoration, they would have found something else. I always regarded the fuss about it as a sort of teapot tempest. If my memory is correct, both the French ambassador and Henry Ford got one at about the same time.

It probably would have been only a "teapot tempest" if the award had been made by another grantor in another country, but this one was by the number-two Nazi, directing a nation that the following year would try to grind the world under its heel. Still, this was not the kind of distinction the apolitical engineer would naturally make, and he did not regard his assignment in his host country as one of forming political judgments. He had come for "just the facts, ma'am."

Visitors to the Forest Park Museum in Saint Louis can see the flying suit that saw Lindbergh safely across the Atlantic in the twenties. They can also see there "the albatross" that just about sank him in the thirties.

There is no question that Lindbergh admired the discipline and vigor of the German nation:

> The Germans are a great people, and I believe their welfare is inseparable from that of Europe. The future of Europe depends upon the strength of this country.

Traveling by train from Paris to Berlin in December 1938, he noted that the immigration officer at the border was:

> . . . a fine-looking type of young German—everything was orderly and efficient. There was an air of discipline and precision which was in sharp contrast to the easy-going pleasantness of Belgium and France.

Some in the media concluded that this type of statement seemed to indicate Lindbergh preferred the vigorous system he saw in central Europe to his own. Anne published a book in 1940 called *The Wave of the Future*. In it she did not claim the new totalitarian systems were superior, but merely that the tired West would have to learn from their vitality in some way. Since at that time her husband was predicting that Britain and France would be defeated, this book, not in the least because of its title, was seen as leaning toward the German ideology. All in all, the combination of elements drove them more and more into a box. In a 1977 network TV interview, Eric Sevareid drew out from Anne her discomfort about that book. Suggesting that every writer is entitled to one mistake, he added, "I guess that was yours."

"It was a mistake," she admitted. "It didn't help anybody. . . . I didn't have the right to write it. I didn't know enough."

Sir Harold Nicolson, British biographer of Anne's father, Dwight Morrow, who was also the Lindberghs' landlord in 1936–1937 at Longbarn, Kent, wrote in his *Diaries and Letters* that, based on his conversations with the man, he had the opinion that Lindbergh "believes in the Nazi theology, all tied up with his hatred of degeneracy of democracy as represented by the free press and the American public."

According to biographer Leonard Mosley, Lindbergh unsuccessfully tried to persuade Sir Harold, through his son and editor Nigel, publicly to apologize. He insisted the charge was libelous. It was not true, he said, that he hated democracy and believed in the Nazis. Sure, he hated the press, but he could not believe the press represented either democracy or the American people. As to Nazism, he had never believed in it. Even when the democratic system sometimes degenerated, he preferred it, and always would, to any other ideology.

It must also be remembered that in the 1930s a number of substantial public figures, in spite of the growing general concern, were trying to give Germany the benefit of the doubt. There was a certain euphoria about the country arising from the Berlin Olympic Games in 1936. Many hoped and prayed that the enormous energy of the National Socialist Party might miraculously find its way into constructive channels. The Oxford Group's Frank Buchman, although he never met the Nazi leader, was trying to remotivate Hitler in an effort to effect such redirection. Columbia University President Nicholas Murray Butler admired out loud the quality of leadership in the totalitarian regimes. Will Rogers wrote with some enthusiasm about Mussolini. In Britain, former Prime Minister David Lloyd-George described Hitler as "the George Washington of Germany." Even Winston Churchill saw possibilities that out of the new regime there might arise a renaissance in central Europe, and said, "If Britain were defeated in war, I hope we would find a Hitler to lead us back to our rightful place among the nations." Charles Lindbergh, while admiring German virility and productiveness, made no such statements. In fact he is repeatedly on record as to the Nazi evil:

> I was stirred by the spirit in Germany, as I had been deadened
> by the lack of it in England and disturbed by its volatile in-
> dividuality in France. But for me, the ideology, the regimenta-

tion, the intolerance, and the fanaticism of Hitler's Third Reich were intolerable in comparison to alternatives that existed.

After the war, in a 1945 address to the Aero Club of Washington, Lindbergh spoke of our need for "integrity, humility, and compassion," adding:

> I must confess to you that I am fearful of the use of power. . . . History is full of its misuses. There is no better example than Nazi Germany. Power without a moral force to guide it invariably ends in the destruction of the people who wield it.

Two years later, in *Of Flight and Life,* he wrote of Nazism:

> Few nations had contributed more to our civilization in the past . . . but [the Germans] had worshiped science. To it they had sacrificed the quality of life. The temptation of scientific powerhad been too much for these citizens. With science they felt they could be supermen; they could rule the earth. . . . In their search for materialistic power, they had set up science as their god, and science had destroyed them.

It is true Lindbergh was intrigued by the many positive qualities of the German people, but he never affirmed the Nazi regime, and he never wanted Germany to win. Indeed, he hoped the Germans and Russians would totally engage and exhaust each other, leaving Western democracies to rebuild the continent without the devastation of war.

Why was Lindbergh in prewar Germany in the first place? In 1936, the American government was frustrated in its attempts to discover what the Germans were really doing in the way of rearmament. The Treaty of Versailles at the close of World War I had forbidden it, but no one believed the defeated nation was abiding by its provisions. American intelligence had formed a fairly clear idea about the arms buildup on the ground, but all efforts to discover air capability were being stonewalled. Major Truman Smith was the senior military attaché at the American Embassy in Berlin, while the Lindberghs were living in their self-imposed exile in England. Smith hit upon an idea. Perhaps the German leadership would be pleased and proud to show off their aircraft accomplishments to the American air hero. Lindbergh was universally acclaimed across all barriers of race, nation, or politics. Although a colonel in the U.S. Army Air Corps, he was not seen as a military person. Major [later Lieutenant Colonel] Smith reflected that the mystique might be influential with the leaders of the Luftwaffe. He invited Lindbergh to Berlin to help with American intelligence.

A patriotic American, a dutiful citizen, and a reserve officer, Lindbergh saw in the invitation something he could and should do for his country. The strategy worked. German airmen were proud to show the distinguished aviator around. In addition, the communications geniuses of the Third Reich undoubtedly speculated that public association with this universally popular legend would improve the international image of the German high command. Consequently, Lindbergh made five inspection tours of German armament installations before the war. He was invited to fly their planes and inspect their factories.

It is not the purpose here to deal with the complicated details of those trips, to whom he reported his findings, and what effect they had on prewar decisions. There are many published treatments of the matter. Details of the assignments in Germany may be found in the memoirs of Truman Smith, *Berlin Alert*. The present account is designed only to show what these activities reveal about the character and attitudes of the man. A television assessment forty years later stated:

> Lindbergh was the pawn in an intricate intelligence game being played by both Germans and Americans. What the Americans wanted to know was the state of the German air force and what the Germans wanted was someone who could warn the Americans, the English, and the French that the German air force was the greatest in the world. Both sides got what they wanted. Only Lindbergh lost.

Some claim the American aviator accepted unverified phony figures from the Germans about their air capability. There is no evidence to support such a charge. According to military historian Col. Raymond Fredette, the British and French gave Lindbergh figures, but the Germans did not. They only showed by demonstration what they had. Anyone knowledgeable about Lindbergh, the thorough engineer-scientist, would be skeptical about a claim that he would take anything on anyone's say-so—particularly in matters as close to his heart and interest as aviation and his nation's security. He never left anything to chance; he would not even enter a strange automobile without checking under the hood and kicking all four tires. Not to double and triple check important figures on the comparative air strengths of the nations would simply be out of character.

A word about Truman Smith. He has sometimes been painted as a kind of latter-day Svengali, who steered the air hero into unfortunate political shoals. It is a flawed image. Although the two were sympathetic with each other's ideas, there was no apparent change in Lindbergh's after they met. Smith supplied the kind of intellectual stimulation, boyish humor, and enthusiasm that the Lone Eagle counted on from a few intimates to lift his spirits. Smith was not your average attaché. When he returned to Washington in 1939 from his four-year tour of duty as air information officer in Berlin, he was placed by the U.S. chief of staff, General George C. Marshall, at the heart of U.S. intelligence. General A. C. Wedemeyer said that if it had not been for his diabetic condition, Truman Smith might have played a role equal to Eisenhower's in the war.

Colonel Smith was a happy man, with a ready story and a rolling laugh. He was mustachioed, handsome, and at six feet four, taller than Lindbergh. An accomplished writer, his military commentaries appeared on occasion in *Reader's Digest,* which he said carried three kinds of articles—Oh the glory of it, Oh the pity of it, and just Oh.

Lindbergh's prewar German experience was one more exciting adventure in an excitingly adventurous life, but it did not help him in the history books. Still, he never showed much concern for public opinion. He always did what he believed he should—and let the chips fall.

And fall they did.

9

Roosevelt and an Achilles' Heel

The report is around Washington that the Administration is out to "get me." Well, it is not the first time, and it won't be the last.

When Wendell Willkie became the Republican nominee for president in June 1940, he announced with some bravado that he hoped the Democrats would, at their convention in July, renominate Franklin D. Roosevelt for a third term in the presidency. He wanted, he said, to "take on the champ." As it happened, the champ won, and Willkie became just one more public figure who was to discover the formidable odds involved in contending in the national arena with the then president of the United States. While advocating a much stronger American defense, Lindbergh wanted to stop America's march toward war. In retrospect, it might be concluded that the country's participation was inevitable. Playmaker Roosevelt apparently had history on his side. People today who compare the 1939–45 conflict with other hostilities of recent decades often call it the "good war."

Lindbergh had two major problems in opposing Roosevelt's intervention policies. First, he was obsessed with the absolute decisiveness of air power, a factor that blinded him to important human and social considerations. Second, he was a political adolescent up against the political genius of the century.

In his first conversation with the president, in April 1939 at the White House, Lindbergh was impressed with the famed Roosevelt charm.

Although there was something about the president he did not quite trust, "Still," he wrote in his diary, "he is our president and there is no reason for any antagonism between us in the [military aviation] work I am now doing."

The two had previously tangled in 1934, when Roosevelt became convinced there was favoritism in the way airmail contracts were awarded to the commercial aviation companies and abruptly canceled the contracts, ordering the mail to be flown in army planes by army pilots. Lindbergh, aware that the public hung on his every word, particularly in matters of aviation, objected. Since his Paris flight, he had been the major force in establishing America's budding aviation industry, and air mail revenue had helped substantially. But his concern was more than just that the White House had attacked his cherished endeavors. An experienced airmail pilot himself, Lindbergh believed that giving such a responsibility to pilots who were untrained for it would result in disaster. He sent a strong telegram of protest to the White House, simultaneously releasing it to the press. Subsequently as he had predicted, the army mail planes began to crash. When public opinion supported his position, the White House had to back down. Roosevelt, at the end of his first year in office, was riding a high tide of popularity. Being bested by a thirty-two-year-old pilot did not fit into his idea of the job description of the president of the United States. Biographer Walter Ross writes:

> Aside from the merits of the controversy, it had been a test of Lindbergh's integrity, prestige, and judgment against Roosevelt's. Lindbergh had been proved right by the grisly results of the Army's attempt to fly the mail. Roosevelt hated people who made him look wrong in public. Therefore he hated Lindbergh—and he never forgot.

Five years later, Lindbergh found himself in the position of taking on the President again. This time, however, the stakes were global.

The differences between the two over the 1939–41 war preparations hardened into animosity, bitterness, and genuine hate. There was no attempt at reconciliation on either side. They preferred, perhaps even enjoyed, enemy status. It was a titanic contest over the destinies of nations. Roosevelt moved politically to silence the aviator's isolationist activities.

He offered Lindbergh a cabinet position, Secretary for Air, which would have given the air corps a status independent of the army— as was done late in the war. Will Rogers had proposed the aviator for just such a post in 1928. But Lindbergh, now locked into an adversarial stance with FDR, saw the gesture for what it doubtless was, a political ploy to shut him up. He hardly gave the president the courtesy of a thoughtful reply. Strange, because he was normally meticulous about common amenities. This might well be explained by the fact that apparently there was no direct offer, written or otherwise, from the White House to Lindbergh himself. In the circuitous way in which much Washington business is done, so as not to get anything on the record too soon, this rather significant proposal was conveyed by word of mouth through Secretary of War Harry H. Woodring to Chief of Air Corps Henry "Hap" Arnold to Major Truman Smith. Smith never took the idea seriously, agreeing with Arnold that Lindbergh would certainly decline, and let twenty-four hours go by before even speaking with Lindbergh about it. The latter dismissed the idea as a political ploy, not really calling for a thoughtful response.

It is interesting to speculate on what might have happened if Lindbergh, even though he may have felt the offer impossible to accept, had gone to Washington and had a frank, perhaps even friendly exchange of political and military views. But by this time, feelings on both sides were strong. Furthermore, the gesture would not have been in the style of the aviator. As he said later, resentments may be a good thing. If a person is your enemy, you might as well keep him an enemy—the harsh clash may some day prove productive.

With the isolationist viewpoint gaining public support, and the Administration's pro-Allies position at a standstill, the president, according to Mosley, decided that

> it was necessary to strike down his opponents before they succeeded in dividing the nation. By destroying Charles Lindbergh, he would leave them thrashing around like a snake without a head, and it was against him that he turned his sword.

Roosevelt chose April 25, 1941, for the strike. His custom was to hold an informal press conference twice a week in his office, with reporters crowded around his desk. In those days, accounts of his remarks were paraphrases; no one was allowed to quote the president verbatim. Stephen Early, FDR's competent press secretary, would often plant topics on which he knew his chief would have something interesting to say. He did so on this occasion. Correspondents in the room asked the president about a recent Lindbergh speech. Since the aviator was a reserve officer, one asked, why was he not called into active service, where there would be no more speeches?

Mr. Roosevelt answered by harking back to 1863 and a Union reserve officer, Col. Clement L. Vallandigham, who opposed the War Between the States and said the North could not win. Adherents of his view were regarded as traitorous, and were called Vallandighams, or more popularly, Copperheads, after the venomous serpent. Twentieth-century equivalent terms would be "quislings" or "appeasers." President Lincoln, it was noted, deliberately did not call up the officer in question, implying that such a person is not an asset to an army. FDR neglected to make the distinction that unlike 1863, the nation was not at war in the spring of 1941, and that freedom of speech is freer in peacetime. His historical allusion also carried the subtle implication that being against Roosevelt was like being against Lincoln.

The inevitable headlines the next day proclaimed:

PRESIDENT CALLS LINDY A COPPERHEAD

Whereupon the aviator resigned his military commission. If the accused had taken time to reflect, he might have seen himself in a stronger position by remaining a reserve officer; but even though his friend Truman Smith advised him not to withdraw, he felt strongly that it was a matter of honor and immediately wrote the president a letter of resignation. Some said it was another example of political naiveté, but Lindbergh was more interested in integrity than political advantage. Also, he had let the president put him on the defensive, and his anger grew. The White House directed the Federal Bureau of Investigation to put him under surveillance, ordering in his case a special exception to the regulation against wiretapping.

Harold L. Ickes, secretary of the interior and sometime presidential hatchet man, wrote to FDR that he had analyzed Lindbergh's speeches and articles and was convinced that "he is a ruthless and conscious fascist, motivated by hatred for you personally and for democracy in general." The poet-biographer Carl Sandburg in June 1941 spoke of "the famous flyer who has quit flying and taken to talking, who is proud that he has ice instead of blood in his veins." Anne called this an unfair attack from "a man who had studied Lincoln's life, who praised Lincoln for remaining true to his conscience, even if every friend left him."

The engines of managed information geared up. In Chicago, as Lindbergh arose to speak at a huge rally, the crowd demonstrated its usual enthusiasm by prolonged applause. He raised his hand both to acknowledge their support, and to encourage them to let him start speaking. When the photo appeared on the street the next day, his gesture looked like a Nazi salute.

To cite Ross again:

> One cannot avoid the conclusion, on balancing the evidence, that Roosevelt built Lindbergh up as a pro-Nazi so he could break him. Lindbergh was a strong and dangerous political antagonist, never a potential traitor.

The aviator's rage against Roosevelt was now at a boiling point, and his frustration was intense. In his address to a mass rally in the Hollywood Bowl on June 20, 1941, he stressed the good-guys–bad-guys theme: "We fight with the blade of truth as our greatest weapon. They use the bludgeon of propaganda." In his speech in Des Moines on September 11, he continued:

> The Roosevelt administration . . . have used the war emergency to obtain a third presidential term for the first time in American history. They have used the war to add unlimited billions to a debt which was already at the highest we had ever known. And they use the war to justify the restrictions of congressional power and the assumption of dictatorial procedures on the part of the President and his appointees.

Americans are used to hearing political opponents use platform language like this against each other. But in the mouth of Lindbergh, the outrage had a special quality.

A dedicated nonorganization man, Lindbergh was so wrought up over the advance of interventionism that he abandoned his deeply held nonjoiner principle and associated himself with the America First Committee, accepting a position on the board. The organization was founded in September 1940 by a multipartisan group of prominent citizens who wanted to keep America out of the war and was headed by General Robert E. Wood of Sears Roebuck. The side of the debate arguing for intervention was being led by the Committee to Defend America by Aiding the Allies, whose chairman was Kansas editor William Allen White. Lindbergh had reservations about the America First group, but they shared his views and gave him a platform and the machinery of public communication. He was their star speaker and drew the biggest crowds. Rallies were held in major cities throughout the U.S. until the attack on Pearl Harbor December 1941.

In the Des Moines speech on September 11, Lindbergh removed all of Roosevelt's worries about his being a threat to the Administration's program. Venting his anger against the President, the Lone Eagle, as in a Greek tragedy, proceeded to destroy himself. Whatever one may have thought of his isolationist politics, in Des Moines he waded into inky racial waters, and from that excursion his public image never recovered.

After weeks of reasoned and unsuccessful argument, Lindbergh concluded the people needed a shock. The shock he proposed was to "name names." He mistakenly thought that if the public were aware that they were being pushed and knew who was doing the pushing, they would resent it and stop it:

> The three most important groups of people who have been pressing this country toward war are the British, the Jewish, and the Roosevelt administration. . . . If we were Englishmen we would do the same. . . . It is not difficult to understand why Jewish people desire the overthrow of Nazi Germany. The persecution they have suffered in Germany would be sufficient to make bitter enemies of any race. No person with a sense of the dignity of mankind can condone the persecution the Jewish race has suffered in Germany. But no person of honesty and vision can look on their prowar policy here today without seeing the dangers involved in such a policy, both for us and for them. . . . Their greatest danger to this country lies in their large

ownership and influence in our motion pictures, our press, our radio, and our government.

The tragedy of that speech is that if he had listened, he could have saved himself the wreckage. He had a practice of showing drafts of his speeches to Anne and sometimes to his friend Jim Newton before he delivered them. This one Jim did not know about until he saw the next day's headlines in Concord, New Hampshire. Anne, however, saw it in advance and sounded an alarm. Pointing to the Jewish paragraph she remonstrated, "You mustn't say that, because you will be called anti-Semitic. You will be considered a man who is carrying the flag of anti-Semitism."

"But I'm not anti-Semitic," he said. "Fix it up so it doesn't say that."

"I can't fix it up. If you mention these groups at all, you're going to be in trouble."

But he gave the speech anyway. Why?

"He was a stubborn Swede," says Anne. Warnings of "trouble" had never affected his decisions before; he was not about to let them start now. He could handle trouble. Although he was reading books, Anne believed he was not reading enough of the kind of current material that could help him realize the public impact of his words. Many Jews have resented the Lone Eagle ever since. Not only were they offended by his lumping them as one group, as if they all felt the same way, some took issue with the claim that there was "large ownership and influence" in the media and the government. Charles Stone, former director of the Lindbergh Historic Site in Little Falls, Minnesota, says that during his eleven years in charge there, he was not aware of any Jewish visitors coming to the park. Yet outside of the one unfortunate, stubborn-minded speech, it is hard to find anything in the man's record that warrants the charge of anti-Semitism. Growing up in the WASP-oriented midwest, he doubtless absorbed various racial attitudes that were a part of the culture of the time and place. But there is no evidence of any bigotry having been carried over into adulthood. He had an engineer's approach to treating everyone objectively. His family had a constructive record, with his father a foremost advocate in Congress on behalf of minority rights and his paternal grandfather leading the enactment of many reforms in the Swedish parliament, including increased rights for women and full citizenship for Jews. On paper, the younger Lindbergh's broadmindedness is clear:

> I took for granted that I would marry a girl of my own Caucasian race, but this was a matter of custom rather than of prejudice. I felt no antipathy toward red, yellow, black, or brown. If I had fallen in love with a woman of another race, I surely would have married her regardless of difficulties that might have ensued.

Daughter Reeve, has responded to the issue this way:

> I don't think he was anti-Semitic. I think he was not careful enough in the things that he said at that time. He was not a politician, not a diplomat. I think he should have known that what he said would have the kind of effect that it did. . . . I feel that many of the people who criticized him had such a background of suffering from which to criticize. . . . My father's reputation is fine with me. I know who he was. I know the great sweep of his life. Trading quotes is too small for the issues at hand.

Some of the early articles that Lindbergh and Carrel wrote about race and genes could fairly be interpreted as bordering on racism. But there is nothing in his record that would support charges of a social bias. The racial issue is muddied because of unsubstantiated rumors in various quarters that Lindbergh had some kind of leanings toward Nazi racial attitudes. Two German incidents argue against such an implication. First, he was more than willing to cooperate with the American ambassador's plan at the Berlin dinner to persuade Goering to ease the oppression on emigrating Jews. He did not see his function as making any political case, but he was willing to be a team player and be a drawing card to insure Goering's attendance. Second, within a month following that dinner, he and Anne abruptly ended their German stay in protest against racial persecution. Charles was angered by the nationwide, government-organized, anti-Jewish pogrom on November 9, 1938. It was the first of what would become a series of organized pogroms, leading to the incarceration and death of millions of Jews. The outbreak was called *Kristall-nacht,* "night of the broken glass," because of the smashed Jewish store fronts. Lindbergh immediately called the German attaché and canceled his plans to stay on. "I will not take a house in a country that does such outrageous things to its own people," he said. That week in his diary he wrote:

> I do not understand these riots on the part of the Germans. It seems so contrary to their sense of order and their intelligence in other ways. . . . My admiration for the Germans is constantly being dashed against some rock such as this.

The Des Moines speech threw the America First Committee, and indeed much of the country, into an uproar. In a sense, the outbreak of war three months later saved Lindbergh and his colleagues. At that point, he no longer had to convince anybody of anything and could wholeheartedly go all out for military victory. He was much more at home building bombers and training fighter pilots than being involved with politics and making speeches.

How could such a thoughtful and modest person commit such an error? Enraged resentment against his adversary may have been the demon that distorted his judgment, blinded his reason, and drove him to say things uncharacteristic of his true self. A Scottish Calvinist speaker was wont to say that sin "binds, blinds, multiplies, deadens, and deafens." Hatred was Lindbergh's Achilles' heel.

He would naturally hope that he would be judged for the broad positive contributions he made to the quality of twentieth-century life—in transportation, medicine, conservation, and personal integrity—and not for some terrible mistake. But as Mark Anthony complains in his funeral oration in *Julius Caesar*, "The evil that men do lives after them, the good is oft interred with their bones."

If only he had listened to his wife.

The Sad Saga of the Press

I am inclined to think that an irresponsible and completely unrestricted press is one of the greatest dangers of democracy, just as a completely controlled press is a danger in another direction.

One of the most tragic aspects of Charles Lindbergh's career lay in his relations with the communications media. Amelia Earhart, the look-a-like flyer, told reporter Adela Rogers St. Johns that Lindbergh "was very naive about publicity." It was the brooding specter that overshadowed his life. He lived like a hunted animal. Countless decisions were made with an eye to artful dodging. "What wouldn't I give," he wrote, "to be able to ride on trains and go to theaters and restaurants as an ordinary person." Page after page of his diaries are laced with explanations of how he took this train, booked that compartment, or drove his car so as not to be recognized. It is said you can run, but you can't hide. Somehow or other he managed to do both.

A lifelong consultant to the U.S. Air Force, Lindbergh was inspecting air bases after the war. When he arrived at the one in Adak, Alaska, he was met by the commanding officer, Colonel Robert L. Snider. The latter was impressed by Lindbergh's modest policy of always hitchhiking with other personnel, even though the Pentagon would gladly have assigned to him his own personal jet, or even a fleet of them. Snider was at the plane to greet his famous guest, who hardly had stepped onto the tarmac when he asked, "Colonel, are there any reporters here?" It was as though a pheasant might ask whether there were hunters nearby.

"Sir, there aren't any reporters within three thousand miles of here."

"Great, this is the place I've been looking for all my life!"

Lindbergh could smell a camera. Jim Newton thinks the reason Charles looked so glum in a photo of Jim and Ellie's wedding—Charles was best man—was that he froze at the sight of the lens. A typical story comes from Frank McGee, then editor of *Pace* magazine, who was temporarily in Saigon on assignment during the Vietnam War. In a hotel lobby one day, he spotted Lindbergh entering. An alert photojournalist, he raised his camera. An equally alert reporter-dodger, Lindbergh pulled his hat down over his face until he was safely out of range.

Time, of course, was on Lindbergh's side. As age changed his features, he was not so recognizable. However, some of this advantage was lost whenever a press photo did appear, as when he and Anne attended a Kennedy White House dinner. With the photo came more pressures, causing new resistance.

The only medium of public communication Lindbergh liked, outside of his prewar radio broadcasts, was book publishing. He was a skillful writer and a Pulitzer Prize winner. With a book he was in complete control. He could say what he wanted, in the way he wanted, without argument, and without having to answer any silly questions.

His overall attitude toward publicity is perhaps best summed up in a letter he wrote in February 1964 to his old friend and Pan Am colleague Sam Pryor. Sam had invited him to a small, off-the-record meeting with a few business executives, thinking it might be of mutual interest and benefit. Lindbergh declined in a longhand letter. Most of his writing was in longhand. (His papers now reside in the Yale University Library):

Dear Sam,

About the Eastman Kodak request, I shall write very frankly. As you know, I like to live and work pretty quietly, at least as far as publicity is concerned. I feel that I have had

enough publicity to last a lifetime, and several reincarnations.*
Unless there is a really worthwhile objective to be gained, I
would rather not have any more publicity. The results of meetings such as you suggest are more time-consuming than the
meetings themselves. In this case, as you say, everything is
"off the record." I probably wouldn't encounter a lot of publicity, but there are always people who want things.

They want you to attend other meetings, to make speeches,
to autograph and return books they send you, to sign slips of
paper for their children, to read a book they think is wonderful,
to visit their factory or summer camp, to write a letter to a
child or an old friend who is ill. There just isn't any end to it,
and one thing leads to another like a chain reaction. I am especially anxious to avoid publicity relating to my current activities
in life. So for this respect, the more I can keep out of newspapers and magazines and off radio and television, the better. I
like to maintain a high degree of personal and family privacy.
I find that otherwise the quality of life declines.

What was doubtless also in his mind, and what he would not say to Sam
in a letter, was that those who came to the proposed gathering would
probably arrive not really to discuss important issues affecting the future,
but to ogle a famous person, so they could talk about it to their friends.

Many celebrities believe they owe something to the public. Most
have worked hard to achieve wide acceptance, and feel they cannot turn
their backs on the masses whom they have cultivated and who have been
so important to their success. This consideration was entirely absent with
Lindbergh. What he did he did on his own, without help from—and even
in spite of—all those people "out there." Public approval meant nothing
to him, and his celebrity status was altogether serendipitous. He felt he
did not owe anyone anything in the way of autographs, handshakes, or
appearances, public or private. As far as he was concerned, all such

---

*He once told this to a reporter and was startled to read the ensuing headline:
LINDBERGH SAYS HE'S HAD SEVERAL REINCARNATIONS.

froufrou was a waste of time and seriously interfered with his quality of life.

Like other high-visibility people—actor Paul Newman says he is one—Lindbergh decided it best not to give any autographs at all, except in a publisher's office on his own books for promotional purposes. "If you sign once," he wrote, "it brings ten more requests. If you refuse the first request, the word quickly gets around." Jerry Burris thought the aviator was rather rigid on the subject. As a child, Jerry lived with his family on Wake Island where his father was a food caterer for Pan American World Airways. Lindbergh's duty as a Pan Am director and consultant took him periodically to the line's various stations around the world. He once landed at Wake in time for a Christmas party for the company's families. During the festivities, seven-year-old Jerry, who would go on to become city editor of the *Honolulu Advertiser,* asked the aviator if he would autograph the *Spirit of St. Louis* page in his airmail stamp collection. No luck. Burris still thinks the man might have made an exception for a seven-year-old boy in the bosom of the Pan American family.

In his weaving and dodging for cover, Lindbergh would sometimes happily get caught. Cliff Robertson, the actor, who is also a pilot, thought he spied Lindbergh in an airport terminal. Cliff knew Bud Gurney, Lindbergh's earliest barnstorming buddy, who later became a senior United Airlines pilot. Making his approach, Robertson asked, "Aren't you Charles Lindbergh?"

"No."

"Oh, I beg your pardon. I'm a friend of Bud Gurney's, and Bud said if ever I ran across Slim Lindbergh, to give him his best."

"Are you a friend of Bud Gurney's?"

"Sure am, for a long time."

"Well then I *am* Charles Lindbergh."

The aviator's problems with the press reflected his problems with people. He could not understand the press because he could not understand what the people wanted, why they wanted it, and why the newspapers did what they did to get it for them. If he had sought help from a communications professional like his friend Will Rogers, the way he sought a top authority in heart surgery like Alexis Carrel, he might have avoided much unhappiness. But he was so extraordinarily competent in so many ways that seeking help was simply not his way. He preferred to tough it out on his own. It must be noted here that not a few journalists, including Will Rogers, Honolulu reporter Pierre Bowman, and *The New York Times* writer Nan Robertson, were appalled by the treatment given the aviator by some of their news colleagues.

Instead of studying the problem of the press and researching a solution, Lindbergh ran and hid, living, as it were, in a split-screen world. In the engineering half of the screen, he tackled problems, and worked hard to find innovative solutions to produce ultimate victory. In flying the Atlantic, for example, he had to decide what to do when a storm loomed—fly over, around, beneath, through, or turn back. Whatever the problem, he was going to solve it or die. It would never occur to him to look at a thunderstorm and say, "It shouldn't be like that." He accepted nature as it is. But he simply could not accept human nature in the same way. In the people/press half of the screen, he gave up the battle in disgust. He was not interested in clarification. With the press he was always saying, "They shouldn't be like that." Solutions became impossible because he abandoned his engineer's exercise of reason. To him, the press was not a problem to be solved but a pain to be avoided.

A close-up on Lindbergh's response is seen in his return to New York after three years in Europe, where he and Anne had fled after the kidnapping trial. In April 1939, he came back by himself on the *Aquitania,* his family to follow later. The Carrels and Jim Newton took a pilot's tender out to meet him.

It is difficult to appreciate the voracious appetite the American public still had for news of Lindbergh. It had been twelve years since he had lit up the world, and the reporters were as clamorous as ever. The only modern comparison would be the Beatles, who at the peak of their visibility were literally prisoners in their hotel rooms and whose individual members today are still besieged whenever they appear in public. Before Lindbergh disembarked in New York, he might have said, "Do they want some pictures and a few words? Tell them I'll give them twenty minutes in the ship's lounge." But he believed reporters were insatiable, and if he gave in once, it would be that much more difficult the next time. The police offered to form a cordon to escort him off the boat, but he preferred to push through on his own.

> At 10:15 I asked Newton to go out and size up the situation. In five minutes he returned and said all of the passengers were off and the gangway clear except for press representatives. He said the boat was jammed with them. We then left the cabin. . . . All the way along the deck the photographers ran in front of us and behind us, jamming the way, being pushed aside by the police, yelling, falling over each other on the deck. There must have been over a hundred of them, and the planks were covered with the broken glass of the flashlight bulbs they threw away. I have never seen as many at one time before, even in 1927, I think. . . . It was a barbaric entry to a civilized country.

Lindbergh's press attitude, it is often said, was shaped by his experience with the newspapers following his infant son's kidnapping and the subsequent Hauptmann murder trial. Although it is by no means the full story, there is some truth to it. It was the conduct of the media during that period that led the couple in 1935 to conclude they could not go on living in their home country. Two especially searing and souring events helped form that decision. The first was when a press photographer broke open the dead baby's coffin. For the rest of his life, Lindbergh saw that man in every news camera. Six years after the incident, he was in Washington for a meeting of the National Advisory Committee for Aeronautics. Before the session began, the press photographers wanted a group shot, but only if Lindbergh was in it. When he gave his standard refusal, they said that if he would allow one photograph, they would let him alone in the future and would give their word of honor. Cold fury leaps up from the pages of his diary:

> Imagine a press photographer talking about his word of honor! The type of men who broke through the window of the Trenton morgue to open my baby's casket and photograph its body— they talk to me of honor.

The other incident that finally precipitated the Lindberghs' decision to move to England involved their second son Jon, at that time their only child. He was three years old and during the trial was kept under armed guard whenever he was out of the house. The Lindberghs moved in with the Morrows in Englewood, New Jersey, where Jon could attend nursery school several blocks away. One day when Jon's nurse was driving him home from school, a car started to pass them, then wedged them to a stop against the curb. A cameraman jumped out, took pictures of the child, who was by now crying, and drove away. That did it. In England the Lindberghs found a different atmosphere. They were relatively undisturbed by journalists and had no need for police protection.

Originally, the aviator worked with the newspapers as a team player. True, he was baffled by their antics from the beginning, but in 1927 he intelligently saw the importance and power of the press in helping to win public support for the advancement of aviation. Strange as it sounded later, he even willingly accepted the services of public-relations experts. Lindbergh? Public relations?

A New York public relations firm run by Dick Blythe and Harry Bruno was handling publicity for the Wright Aeronautical Corporation of New Jersey. The company had a big stake in the upcoming Atlantic attempt because the *Spirit of St. Louis,* like its competitors, was powered by Wright's Curtiss Whirlwind engine. They were consequently not only interested in the success of the plane, but also in protecting the small-town boy from the devouring forces of the New York jungle. Press interest was rising even before Lindbergh left San Diego, and Blythe and Bruno phoned him there with an offer to help. Lindbergh accepted.

Blythe met the young pilot when he arrived in New York, and during the hectic preflight week the two roomed together at the Garden City Hotel on Long Island. They became good friends. The new associate was more than a press agent, although he did help channel pertinent information to the media. He also protected the pilot when needed, looked after Evangeline Lindbergh when she came from Detroit for a brief visit with her son, and, as a break from the tension, initiated a Broadway theater party. On Lindbergh's return from Paris, Blythe was on hand in Washington D.C. to meet the *USS Memphis,* which had borne the pilot and the crated *Spirit of St. Louis* back across the Atlantic. After an hour's visit with his mother in a ship's cabin, he had a conference with Blythe, during which he actually changed his mind because of the public relations man's advice. He had intended to appear in his army captain's uniform, which he had worn, complete with necktie, on his flight across the Atlantic. Dick persuaded him not to, since the flight had not been a military exercise and an army image would detract from the feat's universality. After some resistance, the pilot finally agreed, and when he came down the gangplank he was wearing a blue serge suit. There is nothing to indicate that such an occurrence happened again, but the record shows that there was a moment once when Charles Lindbergh listened to a professional's advice on how to deal with the public.

Although the entire welcome-home operation was an outstanding success and we may assume Lindbergh was grateful to the experienced personnel who helped make it so, he may have thought that such assistance would be unnecessary in the future. His fame, he believed, would be gone within months and he would no longer be a public figure who needed to think about these things. It did not work out that way, of course, and his relations with the information industry became a continuing struggle.

His attitude toward the press was no different after the kidnapping and the trial from what it was before. The antipathy was more intense, but the attitude was the same. Whether the relationship could have been healed if this or that had taken place is mere speculation. Lindbergh's intense individualism was a two-edged sword, contributing to great pluses and great minuses. His wife Anne later told a television interviewer:

> Charles Lindbergh would not take advice, because he never listened to anyone. He listened to himself. He was what David Riesman called an "inner directed man." It was a characteristic that worked for him and against him. This was part of his great genius and part of his great failure. So often we look at a person's virtues and don't stop to realize that his vices are the other side of the same thing. If he had listened to people, he would never have flown to Paris.

Perhaps it is too much to ask of the man that he, or we, have it both ways.

Seeds of Trouble

I suppose if I had any resentment in my life, it would be against the press.

On a sweltering July day on Long Island in 1931, Charles and Anne Lindbergh were completing preparations for imminent departure from the College Point Airport on their intercontinental flight to explore a Northwest passage to Asia. The twenty-five-year-old bride of two years, a Smith College graduate–turned–radio operator, was waiting for her husband and his ground crew to make final adjustments. She was irritated by a nearby radio announcer who was souping up the scene for his audio-only listeners by verbally clothing her with dashing garb—"leather flying helmet and leather coat, and high leather flying boots"—when in fact she was wearing a sticky cotton blouse and thin rubber sneakers with the sun beating on her bare head.

Anne Morrow Lindbergh, the Wall Street banker's daughter, despite her parents' life in diplomacy and education, had lived a sheltered life. The world of press relations was new to her. The kidnapping trauma was still to come the next year. Her husband had probably advised her to say nothing to the press. He believed that the less said to them the better, as they would no doubt get it wrong anyway and use it to cause problems later. Consequently, her coached answer to all questions was, "I'm sorry, I really haven't anything to say." She describes the College Point scene in her best-selling book, *North to the Orient:*

As I walked out of the building two women ran up to me.

"Oh, Mrs. Lindbergh," said one, "the women of America are so anxious to know about your clothes."

"And I," said the other, "want to write a little article about your housekeeping in the ship. Where do you put the lunch boxes?"

I felt depressed, as I generally do when women reporters ask me conventionally feminine questions. I feel as they must feel when they are given those questions to ask. I feel slightly insulted. Over in the corner my husband is being asked vital masculine questions, clean-cut steely technicalities or broad abstractions. But I am asked about clothes and lunch boxes. Still, if I were asked about steely technicalities or broad abstractions, I would not be able to answer, so perhaps I do not deserve anything better.

"No", I said. "I'm sorry, but I really haven't anything to say." (What could I say that would have any significance? All the important questions about the trip will be answered by my husband.)

"But you must not disappoint all the people who are so anxious to hear about you. You know, the American Public—"

(—will be disappointed if they don't know where I put the lunch boxes! You aren't going to ask me to believe that, I thought.)

"I'm sorry, I'm very sorry."

In later years, Anne Lindbergh surely would have shown more sensitivity to the young women reporters, who were perhaps testing journalism as a career and who knew, if Anne did not, that a huge majority of their readers could relate more familiarly to clothes and lunch boxes than to steely technicalities or broad abstractions; that the housekeeping in a ship of newsworthy people was of legitimate human interest; and that popular understanding could well be of benefit to this and future exploratory missions. The brilliant author who was to write *Gift from the Sea,* to which so many women have responded, would probably not in later days have declared that "all the important questions about the trip will be answered by my husband."

Anne Lindbergh would become a gracious communicator with the public through the media. But on this occasion she was being loyal and reflecting the intransigence of her partner. The College Point story, more clearly than any other account, reveals the seeds of trouble—the deep roots of the sad saga of Lindbergh and the press.

In the newsrooms, the aviator's elusiveness made him all the more targetable. Editors stepped up pressure on reporters and photographers to get "something." When frustrated, they fabricated quotes and spliced pictures, such as the composite photo which front-paged him and his mother in a pre-Flight affectionate farewell, even though they had refused the requested pose. "I was furious," he wrote. Each deception made the stubborn Swede all the more disgusted, angry, and determined to shut the hounds out. Some of his best friends, such as the Guggenheims, counseled him to accept the fact that, whether he liked it or not, the reality was that he had become a public figure and would be for some time. They thought he would find it helpful to think through his press relations in that light and perhaps even bend a little in the interest of reducing the pressure. A touch more familiarity, they advised, might breed less contempt, reduce the mystery, and cool the demand. He recognized their care but declined the advice. Public relations was a world he knew very little about, and the less he knew the better. He would have resonated to cartoonist Garry Trudeau's *Doonesbury:* "This is the only country where failure to promote yourself is widely considered arrogant."

Lindbergh's attitude toward reporters was that it was his life, not theirs, and he would talk about what he wanted to talk about, not about what they wanted him to talk about. While others in public life learn to deflect personal questions, the young pilot was angered by what to him was unconscionable intrusion. When a reporter queried him about girls, he replied, "I will be happy to answer that question if you can tell me how it relates to aviation." Another time, when asked whether his wife was pregnant, it looked to one witness as though he would explode.

In his cussed, independent way, Lindbergh was rather proud of his resistance. He and the press were playing an ongoing adversarial game, and he usually felt he was winning. When he heard how pilots and management had reached a solution to a strike at a Miami-based airline after the two sides honestly apologized to each other for their resentments, Lindbergh's reaction was that resentments are a good thing and keep life sharp and interesting. He preferred to hang onto his. The last thing he would do would be to apologize for his animosity toward the press. The news people would just laugh at him, he said, and he seriously doubted whether such would have any effect on their ways.

Beyond his obstinate refusal to adapt to celebrity status, Lindbergh's basic problem with the news industry arose from his resistance to learning what made people in the mass do what they do. Whatever it was, he thought they should not do it. Like King Canute with the ocean, he asked the press tide to recede. When it did not, he did.

Anne Lindbergh has summed up the whole business better than anybody. When it came to the press, she said, her husband was irrational.

12

Don't Call Me—I'll Call You

There are certain things people have a right to know—things they are really told too little about. I feel a little differently about a press relationship where I am taking part in a project of definite public concern.

There were times when Lindbergh moved toward the press. He knew the power of newspapers, and he used it on occasion to advance interests he thought important. Then he *was* Charles Lindbergh. This led one newsman to complain, "It's all right for him to call us, but not for us to call him."

In his autobiography, published in the 1950s, Lindbergh remembered complaining about "the newspapers and the crowds they brought" interfering with preparations for the oceancrossing, and then added,

> But I wanted publicity on this flight. That was part of my program. Newspapers are important. I wanted their help. I wanted headlines. And I knew that headlines bring crowds. Then why should I complain?

He liked one side of the coin but not the other.

> The excesses are what bother me—the silly stories, the constant photographing, the composite pictures, the cheap values that such things bring. Why can't newspapers accept facts as they are? Why smother the flavor of life in a spice of fiction?

There are numerous instances of Lindbergh's using the press, such as his simultaneous release of the text of the telegram he sent to President Roosevelt to protest the airmail contract cancellations. His use of the newspapers helped win that contest.

This practice sometimes backfired. On a later occasion, when he again released to the press a copy of a letter to the White House before the original could arrive by mail, FDR's press secretary, Stephen T. Early, took him to task. It was July 1941 and Lindbergh had written the President objecting to attacks on himself and his patriotism by Harold L. Ickes, the Secretary of Interior. Mr. Roosevelt had Early respond:

Dear Mr. Lindbergh:

. . . The text [of your letter] was in the possession of the Press . . . more than twenty-four hours before it reached the White House. . . . It appeared obvious that you had written the letter for the Press—that you merely addressed it to the President. . . . This is not the first instance of its kind. It has happened before. In keeping with time honored tradition the text of this letter will not be given to the Press, at least until you have received it.

In many ways, Lindbergh understood journalism very well. He had confidence in *The New York Times,* most of whose news he thought was fit to print. When he and Anne decided to move to England in 1935, he called in his *Times* reporter friend, Lauren D. "Deac" Lyman, who had covered the Flight seven years before, and gave him the self-exile story in advance, with permission to share it. The resulting feature earned Lyman a Pulitzer Prize. There were other New York reporters on *The Times,* the *Post,* and the *World*—"a few with standards I respect"—who he thought understood what he was doing in 1927 and reported accurately and fairly. In 1939 he approached Gilbert H. Grosvenor, editor of the *National Geographic,* to suggest an article on Robert Goddard's work with rocketry in Roswell, New Mexico.

When Charles and Anne returned to the United States and entered the anti-war effort, they sought all the publicity they could get. In December 1940, Anne made a radio broadcast over NBC. The next day, her husband hastened to the newsstands, only to be disappointed in the press treatment. He was surprised at his conflicting feelings.

It is strange, our desire in this instance for newspaper attention. For many years we have tried to avoid the attention of the press. For years we refused to speak over the radio, to give statements or interviews, to take part in political meetings. Now, this morning, we are disappointed because Anne's address last night is not carried in the papers on our breakfast table.

"This seeming inconsistency" could be justified, he wrote, by separating the persons from the cause. The couple did not like the "brilliant, burning, hardened spotlight" focused on themselves, but welcomed their role as "objects upon which the light is thrown." If they were treated as but players in the service of the campaign, this was acceptable.

Conservation was a cause for which Lindbergh was willing to cooperate with the press to achieve selected objectives. In 1968, before a joint session of the Alaska legislature, he made his first public address in twenty-seven years. Sam Pryor's daughter, Tay Pryor Thomas (Mrs. Lowell Jr.) had told him they needed media help to save the wolf and other endangered species. Afterwards, the Thomases were pleased with the resulting consciousness-raising in press and public about the Alaska environment.

In 1970, Governor Elmer L. Andersen of Minnesota coaxed Lindbergh into his living room in Saint Paul to talk to key Twin Cities reporters about the governor's aim to establish Voyageurs National Park. He was able to secure the famous Minnesotan's cooperation with the press by convincing him the project would fail without increased media attention. Lindbergh, who believed that parks symbolize "the greatest advance our civilization has yet made," would come, however, only on condition that his name would not be mentioned in advance of the meeting and that in no case were the words "press conference" to be used. The diplomatic governor, whose credibility and prestige carried no little weight, simply told the reporters that his guest was so important they would surely regret missing the opportunity. They came. The national park was ultimately assured.

In 1971, Lindbergh invited another *New York Times* correspondent he trusted, Alden Whitman, to review with him from the air the environmental situation all the way from the Atlantic seacoast to Hawaii. The aviator's writings had been replete with his mounting concern over the creeping environmental deterioration he observed from his flights every year across the country, and he thought this writer could help alert the public to the dangers. Whitman would later write a ten-thousand-word obituary for the aviator in *The Times*.

Near the end of his life, Charles Lindbergh actually did hold a press conference. It was June 28, 1973, the centenary of the birth of his great friend Alexis Carrel. Georgetown University in Washington, D.C., invited Lindbergh to speak. To do so he canceled an engagement in Europe. The press was not allowed at the ceremonies, but following his address, to the astonishment of his friends, he agreed to meet with reporters. Answering question after question about Carrel, he drew the line when they asked about Lindbergh. "We're here for the centenary of Dr. Carrel," he said, "and I'll answer any reasonable question about him, if I can," adding with a smile, "anything else—forget it!" An eyewitness observed, "Throughout the interview he was relaxed and courteous, but firm."

13

Philosophy of Force

A law to be effective must be backed by a police force. But I confess to you, I am fearful of the use of power. Power without a moral force to guide it, invariably ends in the destruction of the people who wield it.

Charles Lindbergh was nothing if not a thinker. Although reading was not his favorite pastime, he read a lot. When Jim Newton told him that Arnold Toynbee's *A Study of History* had come out in an abridged version, Charles said no, he wanted to read all ten original volumes. He was an all-or-nothing type, and besides, the abridger might have omitted parts important to him.

The use of force was a subject that intrigued Lindbergh in both his reading and in his writing. Typically, his complex mind was eloquent at times on one side of the issue and at times on the other. He believed that force was necessary to preserve civilization, but he also wrote that the use of force might well destroy it.

One of his favorite books was Alfred North Whitehead's *Adventures of Ideas*. Whitehead, a world renowned professor of mathematics in Great Britain until 1924, became professor of philosophy at Harvard University until 1936, and emeritus until his death in 1947. Lindbergh responded strongly to the professor's concepts, reminiscent of Carrel's thinking, which rejected mechanical materialism in favor of a subjective idealism, attempted to reconcile science and metaphysics, and viewed the universe as organic. Lindbergh's *Wartime Journals* indicate that he read and reread *Adventures of Ideas* in trains, planes, and hotels. Anxious to meet the professor himself, Charles and Anne in January 1940 made the seven-hour auto trip—to avoid being recognized on the train—from Englewood, New Jersey, to Cambridge, Massachusetts, for dinner and an evening with the Whiteheads in their home. Excerpts from his account:

> Professor Whitehead is all one would expect from reading his books. . . .[He] has a wonderful mind. It was worth many trips to Boston to talk to him. Mrs. Whitehead is also a remarkable person. It is seldom indeed that one finds two such people together. . . . [It was] one of the most interesting evenings I have ever spent. . . . He spoke of the rise of "gentleness" over the centuries. I asked him if he thought it could exist without the protection of "force." He agreed with me that it could not. I was anxious to get his reaction to this, as I came to that conclusion long ago.

This tension between "gentleness" and "force" was a consistent theme in Lindbergh's life and thought. He was dedicated to building through aviation national economic strength and international peaceful understanding. He also devoted a lifetime to service in the armed forces, which he saw as preserving those positive values. His daughter Reeve thinks that for him it was "an ambivalent thing to be flying in a bomber after the *Spirit of St. Louis.*" And he placed all his hardnosed military thoughts in subservience to his antipathy to the actual use of force. He did this for the same reason General Douglas MacArthur did at the Japanese surrender aboard the *USS Missouri,* when the old soldier declared that the utter destructiveness of war blocks it out as an alternative, and said, "We have had our last chance." Lindbergh, too, was worried about a nation's capability of total annihilation—through force unguided by moral responsibility—as in the case of Nazi Germany.

> We may have to resort to arms in the future as we have in the past. . . . But let us have the wisdom to realize that the use of force is a sign of weakness on a higher plane, and that a policy based primarily on recourse to arms will sooner or later fail.

Contemporary experience and a study of history led him to hold that a country had to have arms to keep its freedom, and that a peace treaty required force to implement it. But he was torn between approval of war in the abstract and resistance to it in actual terms. In light of his contesting America's participation in World War II, he has been accused of a sinister desire to remove obstacles to Nazi advances. But the reasons for his opposition may have been more primordial, such as his fear that an Anglo-German war would destroy the continent of Europe and much of Western civilization. Yet he was also outspoken against pacifism. He expressed his inner struggle in the America First days:

> What luck it is to find myself opposing my country's entrance into a war I *don't* believe in, when I would so much rather be fighting for my country in a war I *do* believe in. Here I am stumping the country with the pacifists and considering resigning as a colonel in the Army Air Corps, when there is no philosophy I disagree with more than that of the pacifist, and nothing I would rather be doing than flying in the Air Corps. If only the United States could be on the *right* side of an intelligent war! There *are* wars worth fighting.

He did not name the wars he believed worthwhile. He eschewed his father's pacifism, but may have been closer philosophically to his father than he cared to admit. In many ways, he was still the midwestern farm boy and immigrant's son.

Guns had played a big part in the values of young Charles's boyhood. He owned his first rifle at the age of six, and was imbued with the frontier view of arms as a means of supplying food and protecting one's home and farm. Guns always fascinated him and his mastery of them was complete. Yet when he was invited to go hunting in Mexico in 1928, he accepted the offer only as a cover for being in the country to see his fiancée. "I did not want to kill antelope—or anything else for that matter," he said.

His enlisting in the army had less to do with national defense than wanting to improve his flying skills, but for the rest of his life, he was proud of the time he spent on military matters. Commissioned as a second lieutenant in 1925, he made captain and then colonel in 1927, resigned in 1941, and was later re-commissioned brigadier general by President Eisenhower in 1954. Although he sacrificed his sacred honor and some of his fortune in opposing American entry into the war, after Pearl Harbor he placed his life on the line in commitment to victory. By then he was no longer a member of the armed forces, but managed to parlay a civilian consulting assignment in the summer of 1944 into flying fifty combat missions in the South Pacific. He was there on behalf of United Aircraft Corporation to help navy flyers secure maximum performance from their engines. For him as a civilian to enter combat was illegal, but he rationalized that he could not help the pilots unless he knew first hand what their conditions were in the air. Whether that required fifty missions is another matter. Unspoken explanations might include his personal desire for adventure, plus a felt need to rehabilitate his name by doing some really dangerous fighting at the front. Some writers have said he achieved that result.

As he left the Pacific for the States, Lindbergh told General MacArthur that, through proper engine settings and reduced cruising speeds, he had enabled the pilots to increase their combat flight radius by 50–100 miles—thus their range 100–200 miles—which meant they could reach more distant targets, also having that much added safety margin for their return from enemy skies. In his reflective *Autobiography of Values,* he makes this evaluation of the use of force as experienced in the Pacific theater:

> My combat missions in the Pacific helped to protect the freedom of my country—as the quality of my arms helped to protect me. I felt great freedom of action during those missions, in a combination of individuality and teamwork. There was freedom even in the duel of life and death—his bullets and my bullets, the freedom of life if they passed, the freedom of death if they struck.

When the war was over, he was quoting New Testament prophecy, "They that take the sword shall perish with the sword." Today's sword, he kept reminding the nation, was capable of annihilating the race. There was little satisfaction, he said, in spending one's life developing machines "which are likely to bring ruin to one's own people." He was echoing German rocketry expert Wernher von Braun's observation that science does not have a moral dimension, but is like a knife—in the hands of "a surgeon or a murderer, each will use it differently." Force, Lindbergh said, is a means either good or bad, according to the ends, and ends are a question of motives. Since motives are determined by the moral compass of human beings, he felt it necessary to write about his own. The result was *Of Flight and Life.*

14

Of Flight and Life

I have written this book in an attempt to clarify the crisis we face, to communicate with men and women of similar concern, to search for a solution.

Following the war, Lindbergh brought out what may prove to be the most enduring of his seven books, *Of Flight and Life*. He was forty-six years old. In the volume's fifty-six pages he presents his turning-point testament of faith. A combination of personal journey and worldview, it may some day rank with seminal works like Le Comte du Nouy's *Human Destiny*. There is something of the flavor of Augustine's *City of God*. In it, Lindbergh not only makes his own affirmation of faith, he points to an ideology for the future. The book is a polemic in the best American pamphleteering tradition. Like Tom Paine's *Common Sense*, it was designed to fire hearts to commitment and stir wills to action.

Written just after the atomic holocaust that ended World War II, *Of Flight and Life* describes the terrible danger Lindbergh saw ahead. A modern Paul Revere, he felt an awesome burden to warn the people. He was even prepared to come out of seclusion and use his world celebrity status to help achieve no less a global objective than saving civilization itself.

In addition to the wider perspective he had gained through his reading and his conversations with Alexis Carrel and Jim Newton, the war itself made a change in Lindbergh's thinking. He had counted on the power of science to bring a new level of quality to life, and on the capability of airplanes to speed international understanding and good will. But in the war he saw that science and aircraft had been perverted into the service of terrible death and destruction.

Lindbergh not only outlines the changes he believes are necessary in the world—which many people have done before. He articulates the changes he saw necessary in himself—which few people ever do. These personal changes were rooted in two new outlooks: shifting the object of his worship from science to a transcendent reality above science and adding the resources of the irrational to those of the rational. He said that the worship of God, and living by God's spiritual values, make possible a channeling of science, which in turn, provides material strength to protect spiritual values. Evidence of the changes Lindbergh underwent before and during the war can be seen in a diary note before he left in April 1944 for duty in the Pacific theater. He stopped at a New York bookstore and purchased a small New Testament. "Since I can carry only one book, and a very small one," he wrote, "that is my choice. It would not have been a decade ago; but the more I learn and the more I read, the less competition it has."

In the preface to *Of Flight and Life*, Lindbergh outlines his lifetime goals, saying that on three occasions he had felt an "overwhelming desire" to communicate certain beliefs to others and "to band together with one's fellow men in support of a common cause." These causes, he said, were (I) to advance humankind's great destiny in the air, (II) to keep America out of World War II, and (III) to control science by a higher moral force.

15

A Great Destiny in the Air—Goal I

I devoted my life to planes and engines, to surveying airlines, to preaching, wherever men would listen, the limitless future of the sky.

The screen introduction to the movie *The Spirit of St. Louis*, featuring Jimmy Stewart, proclaims, "In thirty-three hours and thirty minutes the air age became a reality." It did, but it actually took a few more hours to drive the message home. Over the months following the Flight came convincing evidence that here was not only a swift, but also a dependable, new means of moving people and goods. That was Lindbergh's aim for his ninety-five-day, forty-eight-state welcome-home tour from July 20 to October 23, 1927. He landed precisely at two p.m. in eighty-one of the eighty-two American cities he visited. He may have seized the world's attention in May, but the commercial establishment could have written off the flight to Paris as a stunt. Two o'clock exactly in eighty-one cities was another matter. The aviation industry did in fact quadruple in the next two years.

Merrill C. Meigs, the "flying publisher" after whom Meigs Field on Chicago's lake front is named, is but one of the vast array of people inspired by Lindbergh's dream. He was not unlike Lindbergh in appearance—tall, handsome, soft spoken, with an engaging twinkle. He was the Hearst Corporation's vice president for advertising and said that some of the happiest hours of his life were spent at Mr. Hearst's Castle at San

Simeon. Being in the news business, friends would ask him if he couldn't keep it out of the papers that they were found in bed with somebody else's wife. His reply was that the way to do that was not to get *in* bed with somebody else's wife. In World War II, he was put in charge of the War Production Board's Aircraft Division, where he was responsible for securing billions of dollars worth of military planes and equipment. He flew his own plane into his seventies. After the war, he was named to the selection commission that chose the site for the Air Force Academy. Years later, when a friend asked what led him into aviation, he replied, "The day Lindbergh landed in Paris, I said to myself, 'This is the future.' I went out and bought a plane, learned to fly, and have been into it ever since." It is but one example of the ripple effect of the Lone Eagle on countless personal decisions for the air.

Lindbergh's effect on all his endeavors was due in no small measure simply to the way he was and the way he went about things. There was drama in the way he walked. A 1926 photo taken at Lambert Field, Saint Louis, shows the three pilots who were under contract to the Robertson Aircraft Corporation to fly the mail between Saint Louis and Chicago. Suited up and walking, Chief Pilot Lindbergh is a step ahead of the other two. Even the still photo brings out the liquid motion in the six-foot-three frame—an elegance, for want of a better word, in manner. Daughter Reeve says that when her father drove up to visit them in Vermont and went flying with aerial photographer Richard Brown, a member of the family, there was no way of knowing what craft he would be flying, as the rented planes would be different each time. But her mother could tell which one was her husband's by the graceful way he brought his in, with the distinctive moves of a fine dancer or athlete. All this added to his personal appeal, and his personal appeal made aviation appealing.

To this aura of grace was added the attraction of his personal discipline. A higher standard is expected of heroes, and Lindbergh did not disappoint. He did not talk about smoking or drinking. He simply did not like the taste, and he noticed his hands were not as steady on the stick if he even drank coffee. Nor did womanizing figure in his agenda. He noted with detached amusement the other pilots' exploits with the opposite sex, but had no dates himself until the first one with his fiancée. Without any fuss, he made cleanness attractive. Frederick Lewis Allen called him a Galahad, and like the Galahad of old, Lindbergh's popular strength was as the strength of ten because his heart was seen as pure. On the fiftieth anniversary of the Flight, at a dawn ceremony, May 20, 1977, at Roosevelt Field, a former flying colleague, Carl "Slim" Hennicke, used that very word, pure, to describe his friend, the other Slim. Will Rogers wrote in 1929 that Lindbergh had furnished the newspapers "with the only hundred percent clean topic they had in two years." It was a breath of fresh air for everybody, and its magic rubbed off onto the entire aviation enterprise.

Because the major thrust of the space program came too late for Lindbergh's active participation, he had enviously to settle for writing eloquent articles about Cape Canaveral. Verne Jobst, United Airlines veteran, who for years was the official pilot of the *Spirit of St. Louis* replica, once asked Neil Armstrong why was it that the astronauts revered Lindbergh. His reply: "He did it alone; we had a cast of a million." He might have added "and a budget of billions."

Lindbergh did make two major contributions, however, without which space exploration would have been greatly delayed or altered. The first was a pivotal role in developing the rockets that have made the space age possible. Soon after the Flight, Lindbergh began thinking of the possibility of rockets as propellants in future travel. No one he talked to, however, including a specially called meeting of executives and scientists at the DuPont company in Wilmington, Delaware, revealed any knowledge or interest in the subject. On one of his visits to the Guggenheims on Long Island in 1929, however, something happened that he called "one of those unpredictable incidents that so often bend the trends of life and history." Carol Guggenheim showed him an article in *Popular Science Monthly* reporting on an obscure physics professor named Robert Goddard at Clark University in Worcester, Massachusetts, who was experimenting with rockets, and even predicting that some day human beings might escape earth's gravity and reach the moon. Lindbergh at once arranged to meet the professor, drove to Worcester in his air-cooled Franklin car, became convinced the man was for real, obtained grants for him from the Guggenheims, and set him up on a ten-year program in Roswell, New Mexico. There Robert Goddard produced the rocketry that launched the space age. It became another example of the curious and creative turn-of-mind with which Lindbergh was always punching at the big frontiers.

His second, more indirect contribution to the space program was again one where his character played a central role. When the National Aeronautics and Space Administration (NASA) began, the leadership knew public support was essential. One problem they had, which Lindbergh had not, was dependence on federal money, and this required a positive taxpayer attitude. NASA was well aware that the public response to Lindbergh was due in great measure to his personal character, and concluded that the caliber of the person was as crucial as the caliber of the technology. In looking for the first astronauts, then, they set about to find a dozen Lindberghs, candidates who had not only the aeronautical and engineering skills, but were "squeaky clean." They had to have the "right stuff"—and by the "right stuff" they meant being like Lindbergh. This is not to say the program might not have succeeded with a different type of person; it is only to say that Lindbergh had proved that personal integrity was a key to broad-based public support.

Another area where Lindbergh's character contributed to aviation was in selecting the site for the Air Force Academy. On April 6, 1954, Harold E. Talbott, secretary of the air force under President Eisenhower, established a five-member site-selection commission to find the right place for a special academy for air, comparable to those for the other services at West Point and Annapolis. Among the members were Merrill C. Meigs and Charles A. Lindbergh. The next day, by coincidence, the latter was to be sworn in as a Brigadier General in the U.S. Air Force Reserve, after thirteen years of nonmilitary status. The following Sunday, April 11, 1954, the *Orlando Sentinel* in Florida editorialized on the composition of the site committee.

> General Lindbergh's selection disposed of one set of ugly rumors which have been prevalent here for weeks. It was being whispered that Texas had the inside track because the Lone Star state went for Eisenhower in 1952 and that contributions to the

Republican party by wealthy oil magnates were buying the Academy for Texas. The Lone Eagle's reputation for honesty and honor extinguished these rumors as soon as his appointment was announced.

The commission considered 580 locations in forty-five states, fifty-seven of them in California, fifty-one in Texas. Publisher-airman Merrill Meigs was the press spokesman, with guidelines insisted on by Lindbergh—no individual interviews, one group photograph per stop, no civic dinners. Illinois and Wisconsin were among the three finalists, with Colorado Springs announced as the designee June 24, 1954. In his 1988 history of the Air Force Academy, George V. Fagan wrote:

> After his flight over the Colorado Springs site, General Lindbergh concluded that the area was suitable for flying training. This positive pronouncement by one of the world's most famous aviators put to rest the many objections which had been raised both in and out of the Air Force about the Colorado Springs site.

For Lindbergh, the "development of flight" in the "limitless future of the sky" did not necessarily mean routine license for bigger and faster. He had clear ideas about what should not, as well as what should, be done. Tension grew within him between two passions—his desire on the one hand for aviation development and, on the other, his deep concern over its effect on the quality of life. Airplanes depend on an advanced civilization, he noted, but an advanced civilization also means fewer birds. "I realized," he wrote in 1964, "that if I had to choose, I would rather have birds than airplanes."

This kind of conviction led Lindbergh to throw his considerable weight against American development of a Supersonic Transport (SST) in the sixties. The French and British were building the supersonic *Concorde* for trans-Atlantic travel, but Lindbergh told Congress he thought it was best for the U.S. not to subsidize such aircraft, making his case on both economic and environmental grounds. "Seat-mile costs are too high," he said, "and the pollution of the upper atmosphere too dangerous." He was also concerned about the "unnecessary noise" of the sonic boom. The airman's reputation was still such that his voice was probably the decisive factor in America's decision not to enter the *Concorde* competition. He believed the project did not pass the test he projected in a 1972 article in *The New York Times*: "For me aviation is of value only to the extent that it contributes to the quality of the human life it serves."

On May 21, 1987, the sixtieth anniversary of the Flight, a replica of the *Spirit of St. Louis* landed at Le Bourget aerodrome in Paris. At the same moment, from nearby Orly Field, a *Concorde* took off for New York. It would cover the distance in one-tenth the time it took the young pilot in 1927. Because the supersonic craft looked like the logical next step in aviation's six-decade evolution, the American decision not to take that step was hailed as a turning point in the history of flight. Lindbergh was able to persuade the decision makers that progress in the air meant something more than "planes and engines" and "surveying airlines."

That something more was the planet's quality of life.

16

Keep Out of War—Goal II

For five years, at home and abroad, I spoke, wrote, and argued against a fratricidal war.

Lindbergh's second announced goal was to persuade his country to stay clear of World War II. At first this was a popular stand. Public opinion surveys showed that around four-fifths of the American people were against intervention. The Republican candidate in the 1940 presidential election, Wendell Willkie, who also opposed American entry, albeit less strenuously, received more votes than any previous defeated candidate, twenty-two million to Roosevelt's twenty-seven million. Nevertheless, even when popular sentiment began to shift toward the administration's position, the aviator continued to oppose the president's gradual moves. It was another illustration of the pilot's independence and courage; popularity was in no way a guiding light for him. One day in January 1941, Lindbergh arrived in the halls of Congress. He looked strange in that environment, although of course he had walked those corridors with his father thirty years before. The elder Lindbergh had opposed U.S. entry into *his* generation's war, and in the process, sacrificed his political career. Now the son was coming on with a familiar message. Opposed to entry into *his* generation's war, he too was willing to sacrifice reputation for beliefs.

In early 1941, the issue was whether or not Congress would approve Roosevelt's plan to "lend-lease" various American ships and weapons to the Allies, already at war for sixteen months. Since the nation was committed by law to strict neutrality, Lend-Lease would be a variance, requiring congressional action. During a Fireside Chat a month earlier, in December 1940, President Roosevelt had called the United States the "arsenal of democracy," and said we should send "more of everything" —guns, planes, ships—to those "in the front lines of democracy's battle." Prime Minister Churchill was soon to say, "Give us the tools and we will finish the job."

Lindbergh and others regarded all this as carefully crafted language designed to prepare the public for eventually sending American troops. They did not believe Roosevelt's commitment to the contrary. The aviator agreed to be an opposition witness at the hearings on Lend-Lease held by the Foreign Affairs Committee of the U.S. House of Representatives. On the appointed day, Chairman Sol Bloom, a Democrat from New York, brought the session to order and called up the Administration's heavy hitters from the cabinet and industry: the courtly Tennessean, Cordell Hull, Secretary of State; the solid Colonel Frank Knox, Chicago publisher and secretary of the navy; the whimsical William Knudsen, director of what would become the War Production Board. When for the record, the chairman asked the latter's occupation, Knudsen, coming from three years as president of General Motors, replied in his charming Danish accent, "I make things." These headliners, plus lesser knowns, made the case they were expected to on behalf of President Roosevelt.

Then came the opposition with its lead witness, Charles A. Lindbergh. His star quality always lit up every area he entered, and this hearing room was heavily charged—congressmen, reporters, and visitors listening attentively. The committee's ranking Republican was Hamilton Fish, also of New York, and coordinator of the opposition testimony. He asked Lindbergh to take a seat at the table and invited him to make an opening statement if he wished. The witness did and then responded to questions. He had consistently stated his position that the European war was none of our business and not in our interest. In addition, he claimed, the Allies could not win the war even if the United States gave full-scale support. He was to repeat this prediction in later speeches.

When the committee reassembled after a luncheon break, Mr. Fish, who like his star witness was a prominent isolationist, led off in some agitation:

> Colonel Lindbergh, the report of your comments this morning has gone out on the wires, and already the headlines are saying you believe we could not win the war if we got into it. I suppose you are adding: as of now. In order that there be no misapprehension in the public mind, I would like to give you the opportunity of clarifying your position. Do you not believe that if this country went all out, completely mobilizing its manpower, scientific skills, industrial production, and natural resources—that in such a case we *would* win such a war?

Here was a friendly and sympathetic congressman, definitely in Lindbergh's corner, solicitously offering him a chance to take himself off a tough hook. Unfortunately, getting off hooks was not what the man was about. He was oblivious to headlines, misapprehensions, misunderstandings, personal advantage, reputation, public relations—or what people thought. "No, sir," he responded, "I believe that no matter what we did we would not be able to win such a war."

His prediction proved incorrect, of course, but that fact in no way diminishes the raw courage it took for him to stand behind his beliefs. Here was an army man (he still had his commission) telling the top military and political leaders of the most powerful nation in the world, a nation that had never lost a war, that it could not win this one. His wife Anne has pointed out that her husband's basic assumption—which proved false and which distorted his military judgments at the time—was his fixation that air power would be absolutely decisive in World War II. If this assumption had been correct, it would have logically followed that the nation strongest in the air would win. By January 1941 he had concluded that Germany was that nation. He had been consistently advocating, with little success, that U.S. air strength be greatly increased, and he believed the lack of preparation in the Allied countries made them too weak to take on the rapidly accelerating juggernaut.

Such a complex conviction was hardly understandable by the public, and it made Lindbergh an easy target for simplistic attacks from the White House, such as the "Copperhead" burst three months later. His critics concluded, and many still conclude, that if he thought the Germans were so strong, and if he did not want us to fight them, he must have wanted them to win. Again, however, nothing in the record supports such a conclusion. In fact his basic hope was that the totalitarian powers, Germany and Russia, would lock horns in a lose-lose conflict. He wanted the German guns to be pointed east instead of west.

To understand why Lindbergh did what he did in those days, one must again remember that he thought like an engineer. The human element was not his biggest thing. His technical assessments of air strength were accurate enough: the German Air Force was indeed superior to all other air forces in Europe combined. But he was still worshiping science as savior, and had not yet become attuned to the significance of spirit and General Marshall's assessment that morale had become six times as important as materiel. Lindbergh seriously underestimated the levels of moral nobility to which human beings rise in extreme situations. He failed to factor in the love of freedom that empowers ordinary people to do extraordinary things. He misjudged the stubborn determination and character of the British people in their "finest hour." He did not allow for the rallying oratory of Sir Winston Churchill.

Nevertheless, even in his mistakenness, Lindbergh showed again on that witness stand the striking bravery it took to tackle the Atlantic ocean. Historian Wayne S. Cole put it this way: "Lindbergh had as much courage in public affairs as he had always had in the skies. And he proved ready to pay the price."

On December 8, 1941, the United States declared war on Japan. Hitler straightway declared war on the United States. Immediately, America's two most articulate antiparticipation voices changed. Senator Arthur H. Vandenberg of Michigan, who, as ranking Republican member of the Senate Foreign Relations Committee, had been the foremost congressional isolationist, announced:

> I have fought every trend which I thought would lead to needless war. But when war comes to us, I stand with my Commander-in-Chief for the swiftest and most invincible reply of which our total strength may be capable.

The next day, December 9, Lindbergh issued this statement:

> We have been stepping closer to war for many months. Now it has come and we must meet it as united Americans regardless of our attitude in the past. . . . We must now turn every effort to building up the greatest and most efficient army, navy, and air force in the world. When American soldiers go to war, it must be with the best equipment that modern skill can design and modern industry can build.

Nevertheless, even after the war was over, Lindbergh continued to insist he was right all along. Among those who still resent his stance are many of the British. In the terrible days of the Battle of Britain in 1940 and beyond, when the German blitz was leveling large areas of London night after terrible night, and they faced the believable possibility of the first invasion of their island since William the Conqueror, they were receiving word from America that Lindbergh was predicting their defeat. From a platform in New York on April 23, 1941, he said, "It is now obvious that England is losing the war." Many Britishers have not forgiven him to this day. The only glimmer of regret the fallen hero showed came in a 1973 letter to an Englishman he had not seen since 1941. In it he guessed "there were times" when "I said too damn much for my own good."

In achieving his first goal, to develop aviation, Lindbergh was a spectacular success, and his reputation soared. In failing to achieve his second goal, to keep America out of war, he was also spectacular, and his reputation plummeted. His third crusade, to help give science moral direction, was still to come.

17

Moral Control of Science—Goal III

We are in the grip of a scientific materialism which will ruin us tomorrow. I believe the values we are creating and the standards we are now following will lead to the end of civilization.

Lindbergh follows this stark analysis in *Of Flight and Life* with a remarkable confession of faith. He describes his own personal metamorphosis in the years before and during the war, and he shows that the change he is so urgently calling for—to move beyond materialistic values as the saving grace for civilization—was not only a conclusion of his mind, but an experiential happening in his own heart and soul.

> I grew up as a disciple of science. I know its fascination. I have felt the godlike power man derives from its machines. Like most modern youth, I worshiped science. . . . Now I have lived to experience the early results of scientific materialism. I have seen the science I worshiped, and the aircraft I loved, destroying the civilization I expected them to serve.

He was concerned over the destructive bombers he had helped turn out at Willow Run, which would be raining death on innocent city dwellers, and he was reaching for a balance to materialistic science. In a note to Henry Ford on the automaker's seventy-ninth birthday, July 30, 1942,

Lindbergh wrote:

> You combine the characteristics that I admire most in men—
> success with humility, firmness with tolerance, science with
> religion.

"Man has enthroned the idol" of scientific materialism, he declares in his book, "and turned his back on God." To deal with the resulting destructiveness, he points to a possible answer.

> To progress, even to survive, we must learn to apply the truths
> of God to the actions and relationships of men, to the direction
> of our science. . . . We must draw strength from the forgotten
> virtues of simplicity, humility, contemplation, prayer . . .
> beyond science, beyond self.

It is not clear how close Lindbergh came to reaching his third goal—to give science moral direction. In the great social questions, diagnosis is considerably easier than cure. He compellingly articulates the problem and the need, and he does so in his distinctively eloquent literary style. Follow-through, however, is something else again. It must also be said that accurate identification is essential in tackling any problem and is an important contribution in itself. Correct diagnosis is necessary to correct surgery. "There is nothing more practical than a good theory." So if his analysis pointing to a need to answer scientific materialism is correct, even if he does nothing but hand us the torch, he has helped light us on our way.

After writing *Of Flight and Life,* Lindbergh apparently abandoned his concern for the regeneration of human nature and concentrated instead for the rest of his life on the rejuvenation of physical nature. The truth is he was really more at home resuscitating an endangered rhinoceros in Borneo than reorienting an endangered human being in Ohio. The world of nature, from the days of the farm on the upper Mississippi, had always been a friend. The world of people, from boyhood on, had always been an enigma. One may properly argue that since our surroundings unavoidably shape us, improving the quality of environmental nature cannot help but improve the quality of human nature. But such a focus makes human nature a byproduct rather than the main point. To "control our science by a higher moral force" requires adaptation by human beings, the only creatures capable of either moral or immoral force. Not knowing what to do about breaking "the grip of scientific materialism," and apparently finding no one with whom he cared to band together "in support of a common cause," Lindbergh shifted his focus, revising his third goal more aptly to fit his own nature.

After his death, Anne talked about her husband's three "crusades." She spoke of the proaviation and antiwar efforts as delineated in *Of Flight and Life*, but her version of the third goal was different. Instead of repeating his written words that it was to "control our science by a higher moral force," she articulated the de facto revision—the goal she actually saw him pursuing—and said his third "crusade" was to "improve the quality of our earth." Actions speak louder than words, and she was reporting what he in fact did, which was to throw himself into conservation.

Although he had worked through three degrees in the Masons in Saint Louis in 1926, Lindbergh afterwards became an inveterate nonjoiner. Great causes, however, call for exceptions. In aviation, he had founded and joined commercial companies; in antiwar, he had signed up with America First; and finally in earth healing, he affiliated himself with the World Wildlife Fund, the International Union for the Conservation of Nature, the Nature Conservancy, and the President's Citizens' Committee on Environmental Quality. He was keenly aware that he had led the world in penetrating the planet's fragile envelope of air, and he acted like a man doing penance. If amends were indicated, he would do what he could to preserve the envelope and its contents. He was instrumental in saving a number of endangered species on the land and in the sea. He helped establish the Lindbergh State Park in Minnesota (on the old family farm, and named for his father), as well as the Voyageurs National Park on the Canadian border. He also helped extend the Haleakala National Park to Maui's eastern shore.

These kinds of efforts can be enormously important in the regeneration of the human spirit, renewing people's connection with the earth, and helping them find keys to spiritual health and physical survival. They do not, however, generate "a higher moral force" that can "control our science." Part of Lindbergh's problem was that he found it difficult, often repulsive, to "band together with one's fellow-men in support of a common cause," and to communicate "with men and women of similar concern to search for a solution." In aviation, the excitement overcame his tendency toward isolation. In the antiwar drive, he felt so strongly that he gritted his teeth, held his nose, and waded in. But tragically, he never found a group of like-minded people with whom he could "band together" for what may have been the most important of his three goals, at least in its long-term implications for the planet. When Jim Newton introduced him to the Moral Re-Armament program, earlier known as the Oxford Group, a world force dedicated precisely to answering materialism, scientific or otherwise, he expressed some interest and support:

> It certainly attracts a good type, and it brings out an enthusiasm such as I have only seen in the early days of aviation. . . . But they are trying to place everybody and everything into a movement, instead of the other way around.

When in 1939 he first met Frank Buchman, the program's initiator, his response was mixed:

> I was more impressed by him personally than I had been by the radio speech. . . . He has a certain magnetism and openness, and I felt that he was sincere and honest in all he was doing. . . . I still cannot understand what it is in his "movement" that brings out such devotion and enthusiasm in his followers. Nevertheless, with all my reservations, I believe it is a constructive movement at this time and under present conditions.

In 1942, when Lindbergh was building bombers with Henry Ford, the auto maker invited Buchman and an MRA team to stage their presentation "You Can Defend America" for Ford's naval station trainees. Lindbergh chauffeured Buchman on the occasion.

> He sees what is happening to the country more clearly than most people. He realizes that something is seriously lacking in our character and spirit and is trying to do something about it. But his movement has always seemed to me to lack a tangible philosophy and strength. . . . Still, these people are definitely on the constructive side of life and deserve encouragement, at

least until something better is brought forward. As Whitehead says, "Life consists of a choice of alternatives—the better or the worse," and the people in the Buchman movement are undoubtedly one of "the better."

Apparently Lindbergh felt a kinship with the aims of MRA, but took exception to those behind it except for his friends Jim Newton and Carol Guggenheim. It is doubtful he demanded the same kind of perfection of the America First Committee with which he associated to reach a common objective, whatever its faults. But then, one tends to be more tolerant of shortcomings in a political movement than in a spiritual program.

In 1939, Charles had invited Jim to his house on Long Island to help Jim write an article about Moral Re-Armament for *Reader's Digest.* As noted earlier, he hoped his friend would become "a strong and constructive force in the religious rejuvenation of this country." Although the piece never appeared, one suspects that many of the ideas they considered for Jim's prewar article appeared later in Charles's postwar book, *Of Flight and Life,* whose central theme was the religious rejuvenation of the country. Newton wrote in his memoir, *Uncommon Friends,* "I had always felt certain passages in his *Of Flight and Life* were some of the best expressions of MRA ideology I had seen."

In 1961 Charles accompanied Jim to yet another international Moral Re-Armament conference, this time at Caux, Switzerland, above Lake Geneva. "I'd go anywhere for you," he said. Although he praised the message of the dramatic presentations and met there a Masai warrior from Kenya, John Ole Konchellah, who from then on would be the pivot of Lindbergh's ten visits to East Africa, he wrote to Jim afterwards that the program was not for him. One difficulty he probably found at Caux was an MRA tenet that a key to teamwork is honest apology. This was uncomfortable territory for the Lone Eagle.

But over and above such a consideration, as Jim points out, "Charles was too independent to want such an association. He shied away from any association except on his own terms." There is in fact no suggestion in *Of Flight and Life* or anywhere else that he really wanted "to band together with one's fellow-men in support" of encouraging changes in human nature to help save civilization. Perhaps he felt his responsibility ended with writing a book.

What Lindbergh is actually calling for is nothing less than a spiritual revolution of heroic proportions throughout the globe. He may have been thinking of something akin to the Great Awakening of New England 1735–1750, when whole communities and regions took on a new orientation. According to some scholars, that spiritual firestorm laid the psychic base for American independence, leading John Adams to say, "This radical change in the principles, opinions, sentiments, and affections of the people was the real American Revolution."

Lindbergh had doubts whether people will do what is necessary, whether "our follies," as he said, will permit civilization "to advance." Yet he sees hope.

> The answer lies in that quality with which man only, of all earthly life, is gifted. In each person is a spark able to kindle new fires of human progress. . . . This ember may lie dormant through centuries of darkness or it may be fanned to flames by the winds of crisis, sweeping over the earth, bringing others to life with its light and warmth.

His is an appeal for widespread regeneration of moral values in personal, vocational, and political life. And it is a call for nothing short of a new type of human being. "The critically important fact that modern man is beginning, vaguely, to realize," he wrote to a congressional science committee, "is that major changes in his thought and action are essential." A student of Arnold Toynbee, Lindbergh would probably say that if even a "creative minority" moved in these directions, materialistic science would be significantly challenged. Like the sages of old, this latter day prophet is warning us that the alternative is disaster, and like his great-grandfather, is preaching hellfire and damnation to those failing to heed.

> Without this control, without this balance, our military victories can bring no lasting peace, our laws no lasting justice, our science no lasting progress.

Our salvation, and our only salvation, lies in controlling the arm of Western science by the mind of a Western philosophy guided by the eternal truths of God.

In the long perspective of history, if the future does indeed allow us long perspectives, Charles A. Lindbergh may be seen as having provided some of the most important insights of our time.

18

The Maui Hideaway

In the end I found time for solitude and contemplation midway across the North Pacific where space, time, and life interlace the Hawaiian chain of islands, uniquely on the volcanic island of Maui.

In 1967, Lindbergh finally accepted the repeated invitation of his good friend and Pan Am colleague Sam Pryor to visit his retirement ranch at Kipahulu, eleven miles south of Hana at the eastern tip of Maui. Samuel F. Pryor, Jr., had been executive vice president of Pan American World Airways for twenty-eight years, and along with Lindbergh and others, had helped Juan Trippe build it up to become the world's foremost international air carrier.

When Lindbergh finally stopped in Hawaii on his way back from the Philippines to visit Sam, he stayed overnight in the Pryor guest cottage down by the sea. The next morning, walking up to the main house for breakfast, he said, "Sam, this is just what I've been looking for. Do you think there is any way I could get some land to build something on?" Pryor gave Lindbergh five of his fourteen acres. The way Sam told the story, Charles asked, "What do I pay you?"

"You've already paid me," Sam replied.

"What do you mean?"

"Those twenty-five dolls you brought me from Paris."

123

On one of his many trips to France, Charles had secured a rare collection of valuable nineteenth-century mechanical French dolls, which he brought back as a gift to the Pryors for their ten-thousand-doll collection in Greenwich. A friend asked Sam, "Were his twenty-five dolls and your five acres comparable in value?"

"They were to me," he replied.

Charles and Anne built a primitive, no-electricity, alpine A-frame cottage on the ocean, somewhat along the lines she had envisaged in her meditative essay *Gift from the Sea*. The couple resided at their Kipahulu home for around six weeks at a time, about twice a year, according to John Hanchett, the then cattle foreman at the Hana Ranch, who kept the Lindberghs' Land Rover for them between visits.

To appreciate Lindbergh's life and death in Hawaii, one must understand his confederacy with Sam Pryor. The former was a lifelong consultant to, and director of, Pan American World Airways, having laid out the line's original international routes. The latter was the company's political and public relations magician, who kept the U.S. Congress favorable and cajoled emirs, sultans, and chiefs of state for intercontinental landing rights. From his home base in Connecticut, he was also a power in the Republican party and in 1940 ran the national convention in Philadelphia that nominated Wendell Willkie for president. During World War II he was assigned by Trippe, under the company's contract with the government, to construct fifty-six military airports around the world, many of them by converting Pan Am sealane strips.

Sam had a short man's feisty attack on life; he was a winning boxer at Yale and a friend and sparring partner of heavyweight champion Gene Tunney. For a time he was an operative with Interpol, the world police network, and one of his proudest boasts was that he apprehended the drug lord dramatized in *The French Connection*. (The book is dedicated to Sam Pryor.) As a name dropper he was unabashed but quite sincere; he really did know most of the rich and famous of his time. With pride he would inform visitors that his uncle, Edward B. Pryor, as president of the State National Bank of St. Louis, approved the $15,000 loan in February 1927 to help Lindbergh start building his plane. (The bank's vice-president, Harold Bixby, who suggested the name *Spirit of St. Louis,* raised the funds to repay the loan.)

When Sam and his remarkable partner, Mary Tay Pryor, retired from their home in Greenwich, Connecticut, to their new home in Kipahulu, Maui, they discovered that the small missionary church nearby was in ruins. It had been built in the 1860s by Hawaiians and Congregational missionaries from Connecticut and christened Palapala Ho'omau, Church of the Eternal Word. The name—*palapala,* writing; *ho'omau,* forever— reflects Isaiah's declaration, "The grass withers, the flower fades; but the word of our God shall stand forever." The church flourished until 1924, when the local sugar mill closed and the population moved out.

Sam and Mary Tay were dedicated Episcopalians back home, but on the Hana Coast, as in much of Hawaii, the Protestant churches were Congregational, which was the denomination that sent the first missionaries to the Islands. Whether or not the Pryors were commissioned from on high to "repair my church" à la Saint Francis at Damiano, they restored it completely, even to importing period candle-lighted chandeliers from Connecticut. Since 1980 regular services have been held.

Near the "Kipahulu Ranch" sign that marked Sam's driveway, he had mounted another with an inscription he had seen in Darjeeling, "If there is a heaven on earth—it is here, it is here, it is here." One day not long after the Lindberghs came to Maui, Charles and Sam were out for a walk, when Charles said, "Sam, where are you going to be buried?" Sam replied that he and Mary Tay were restoring a dilapidated church a half mile away and they were planning to be buried there. "I'd like to see it," said Charles. When he did, he not only made arrangements for a Lindbergh lot with the owner of the church property, the Hawaii Conference Foundation of the United Church of Christ (Congregational); he also helped with the restoration.

After Charles died, scrappy Sam managed to get himself into local rows. In his gregarious way, he encouraged people to visit Kipahulu, and thought they should have the privilege of paying their respects to the world hero who was also his good friend. His neighbors, who had moved to Kipahulu for the same reasons the Lindberghs did, including to get away from it all, saw Sam's activities as a threat. They kept shutting the gate at the top of the church road; he kept opening it. There was generous profanity and near-combat at the scene, plus legal action over ownership of the road. All the while, Sam was visiting the church daily to ring the bell at 3:00 p.m., and talking with gravesite visitors. As he was leaving the church one day, he reflected that, in the spirit of "love your enemies," he should apologize to his chief antagonist—not for his position, but for his attitude. A measure of peace was restored, and one of the Lindbergh family told a mainland friend that things had quieted down.

Besides his love of the flora and fauna, one of the reasons Lindbergh was so pleased with living on the Hana Coast was that people left him alone and allowed him to be himself. Said one resident, "The people never asked of him anything he did not wish to give." Some remember him pushing a grocery cart around Hasegawa General Store, possibly the only place in the world where Charles Lindbergh could have pushed a cart around a store. A local policeman remarked, "To see Mr. Lindbergh in Hana, you would think he is just some old guy that lives out here. Unless you actually knew who he was, you would pass him on the street and not even say a thing."

There were exceptions. Charles and Anne were sometime dinner guests of Tony and Alberta deJetley, managers of the Hana Maui Hotel, the only inn within seventy-five miles. Sam was a director of the ranch and hotel, and the Pryors were cohosts on these occasions. One evening a matron who had had her full quota from the bar draped her arms around Lindbergh and slobbered, "My hero!" In disgust he got up and started walking home, eleven miles away. "That awful woman," he called her later in a note. The local policeman, who did not recognize him, was curious about someone walking the dark road at night, and asked whether he could help. Lindbergh had found that sometimes a nonsensical remark would shake people off, and said, "The town is over that way." By then the cop probably knew who he was. Charles felt badly about his stiff-arming someone who genuinely offered help and asked Sam to explain to the policeman and apologize. Apparently he felt he could not have done such a thing directly.

For transportation on the rough Hana Coast roads and the cross-country trails into the uplands, Charles asked ranch foreman Hanchett to find for him a four-wheel-drive Land Rover like Hanchett's. The cattle man located a used, fire-engine-red one on Hawaii (the "big island"). Charles asked that it be repainted dark green so as to be less disturbing to the birds he wished to observe in the woods.

Hasegawa General Store has been a landmark institution in Hana for generations. A popular song decades ago made it nationally famous. In the front area were T-shirts ("I survived the Hana Highway"), groceries, postcards, film, and nostrums—displayed in a riot of disarray. In the back was a warehouse where there was to be found a wide variety of brand-name tools, stereos, paint, nails, chain saws, and barbed wire. Only Andy Oliveira, veteran stock clerk of thirty years, knew where everything in that welter was. Harry Hasegawa, whose grandfather started the store in 1910, is the third-generation Japanese family to have run it. Harry's son Neil, a Redlands University graduate, represents the fourth.

Lindbergh, like everyone else in eastern Maui, frequently visited Hasegawa's. When he first arrived on Maui, he asked Harry whether he could look around the place, particularly the warehouse out back, to identify what he would need in the way of tools for survival in the bush. Harry said, "Of course," asking only that he please turn off the warehouse light when he was through. "Invariably," Harry reported, Lindbergh would throw the wrong switch and douse the light in the front part of the store. "At least we always knew who was back there," Harry said. Granted that the word "invariably" could be an exaggeration, still it is of some comfort to know that the most famous engineer in the world was capable of hitting the wrong light switch.

The Lindberghs made good friends within small circles among both the *haole* and the Hawaiians. The Hawaiian word *haole* (pronounced "howly") originally meant "any one coming from some place else." Now it has come to apply only to Caucasians. Among this group, the Lindberghs spent many a happy evening with not only the Pryors, but also the David Grays and the Milton Howells. Dr. Howell, the only physician on the island's eastern coast for a quarter of a century, had also come out of Minnesota, where he had been the mayor of Glencoe. He met Lindbergh in Hawaii when the two worked with Laurance Rockefeller, Arthur Godfrey, Tap Pryor, and others on the Nature Conservancy project around the Seven Pools (*'Ohe'o Gulch* in Hawaiian), resulting in the area's incorporation into the Haleakala National Park.

At dinner parties, Charles would sometimes ask that the doctor's wife, Roselle, be seated next to him, but she admitted she could never get her mind past the celebrity aura and be natural with him. The Grays were also sometime dinner hosts to the Lindberghs, and later provided their home as a haven for Anne on the day of Charles's funeral, allowing her to stay behind the scenes before ushering her down a back way to the church at the last minute. David Gray is a pilot and former Oahu advertising executive, with homes in Honolulu and Kipahulu. He is founding president of the Kipahulu Community Association, which was organized to keep the area, given the presence of a national hero's grave, as peaceful as possible.

Lindbergh felt particularly at home with the Hawaiians. Worldwide he was always drawn to indigenous peoples. Through them he tried to learn what human beings are like underneath, uncorrupted by the artificialities of civilization. He made many trips to East Africa to live with the Masai in Kenya, who found Lindbergh to be "much like the Masai." He was also a frequent dweller with the Tasaday tribe in the Philippines. In Hawaii, Charles's great friend was Joseph Kahaleuahi, who lived in Kipahulu with his wife Annie and their numerous children and grandchildren. Tevi, as he was called, was tall and slim, with lava-black skin, a great smile, and a figure not unlike Lindbergh's. The two would go swimming together in the sea, and bring back crabs and lobsters. A superb artisan, reputedly able to do anything in construction, Tevi built Anne's writing cabin in the woods above the house and at the end dug Charles's grave. At a Christmas luau in Kipahulu, someone asked Tevi how he came to be the one to do all these things for Lindbergh. He grinned and said, "Because he was my friend."

One day Tevi's wife Annie was walking with her grandchildren between her house and the Lindberghs'. When some of them ran ahead, Annie, embarrassed to see they were getting close to the neighbors' cottage, tried to corral them. Starting to remonstrate, she saw Charles smiling down from his upstairs sun deck. "That's all right, Annie," he said, "you and all your family are welcome here anytime you want to come. Only if you have any *haole* friends, don't bring them." Most *haole* wanted something from him; the Hawaiians made no demands.

After her husband died, Anne sold the cottage and continued living in Connecticut. But on that island in the Pacific, the Lone Eagle had found a home where he could preserve his core and promote quality in life—always his Holy Grail. And there at the last he found the runway for his final takeoff.

19

The Lone Eagle's Last Flight

Do you think I am dying well?

In the years after Lindbergh's death, transport pilots on their descent toward Honolulu would tell their passengers something like this:

Over there is the island of Maui. You remember Charles Lindbergh, who as a young man flew alone across the Atlantic Ocean. On Maui he made his last landing. And when we fly over, we remember him.

During Charles's final week, Anne conversed with John M. Tincher, the local minister, who in a few days would conduct the burial service, causing his name to be flashed on the news wires around the world. He asked how her husband was taking the experience. She replied, "Well, he has been close to death so many times, this is for him another adventure—perhaps the greatest adventure."

Her husband had used those words himself. In December 1939, he had been asked by a friend to visit a former associate he had liked and respected. Major Barry had been secretary-treasurer of TAT before it was TWA and was then in a New York hospital dying of cancer. When Lindbergh arrived that evening, Barry's family told him the patient did not know the hopelessness of his case. That night Charles wrote in his diary:

131

Personally, I would prefer to know if I were going to die. I would not want to be misled. It is impossible to know with certainty how one would feel under the actual test of approaching death, but I do not believe I would fear it, and I would want to know of the meeting in advance. It is the last, and possibly the greatest, adventure of life.

Lindbergh thought that what science said about death—virtually nothing—was totally inadequate.

Theology's acceptance of a spirit surviving death is more plausible than the nonentity that one infers from science. Only by dying can we continue living. When man's intellect has gained wisdom, we will welcome death as we welcome birth, both as achievements in a spiral—supporting and completing one another.

As a young man, Lindbergh thought death was terrible. Something should be done about it. At the end he told Anne, "It's not terrible—it's very easy and natural." He thought this time his nearness to death was different from his other experiences because in those there was always something he could do. Here there was not. He had written that death seemed a desirable phenomenon, "a part of a cosmic plan that lay above man's wisdom." He saw the life cycle as needing death and decomposition, and looked at departure no longer as an ending but an opening, like a Maui stream flowing from one pool to another. "Mortality is no concern of rivers and gulls," he wrote. "Neither matter nor lower animals consider that life ends. Only man is aware; only he is disturbed by such a concept."

During the summer of 1974, Lindbergh's lymphatic cancer was worsening, and he was confined for twenty-seven days in the Columbia Presbyterian Hospital in New York. Reeve speaks of her last visit with her father:

He was very ill. He was able to sit up. He was writing. Next to his bed was a little table and a pen and pencil. He was always writing down what he thought about. What I saw on the little blue pad was this whole line: "I know there is infinity outside of us—I wonder if there is also infinity within."

When the doctors finally told him there was nothing more they could do, that it would be a matter of days and they would keep him comfortable, their patient said, "Then I want to go home to Maui." The suggestion met with a strong protest from the medical team. They claimed he would not receive proper care and implied that such a trip might shorten his life. Besides, they argued, as a medical researcher himself, he was part of the system; if he ran out and "abandoned medical science," he would, as the British say, "let down the side." Lindbergh's answer was that they had told him he was not contagious and there was nothing more science could do. "So it is no longer a medical problem," he contended, "it is now a philosophical problem. I would rather spend one day on Maui than thirty days in the hospital."

To release him required that a doctor certify he was fit to travel. He was not, of course, but of the eleven physicians present, one eighty-two-year-old medic agreed to sign him out. The patient had made up his mind, he reasoned, and would find some way. From his hospital bed, Lindbergh called Dr. Howell in Hana to explain his plan. Like the New York doctors, Howell also tried to dissuade him, and with equal success. The patient's Kipahulu home was a dozen very rough miles south of Howell's office. "It is too far away from your medical clinic," said Charles, "for you to take care of me," suggesting a closer place be found for him to stay. The Howells talked to their friends Ed and Jeannie Pechin, who lived in Pu'uiki, just four miles south of Hana. The Pechins had retired there from Wilmington, Delaware, where Ed had been a DuPont executive. They offered their guest cottage to the Lindbergh family for the duration—a truly Hawaiian place on a bluff above the sea.

Sam Pryor wanted to charter a Pan Am plane for the trip from New York and was upset that he could not raise anyone on the weekend. But Charles would not hear of special treatment anyway. He and Anne took the next scheduled non-stop flight on United Airlines from New York to Honolulu, taking up extra seats for the stretcher.

Two days before departure, Charles asked his friend Bill Jovanovich, the publisher, "Do you think I am dying well?"

"Yes," was the reply.

"That's good," said Charles. "You would know."

Two sons, Jon and Scott, joined their parents at Idlewild. Land flew from Montana to meet them in Honolulu, where an ambulance plane had been arranged for the final hop to Maui.

Howell had learned two years previously about the diagnosis of lymphosarcoma. In consultation with the New York doctors, he had administered chemotherapy and medication in Maui. When the ambulance plane landed at the small Hana airport, Charles said to Milton, "It is understood why I have come here, isn't it? I know I have only a short time to live. I don't want anything unnecessary, any heroics." Howell says that from the beginning Lindbergh wanted help to make his death "a constructive act." Throughout their friendship, Charles had called him "Milton," but during this last week it was "Doctor Howell." The patient encouraged the physician to write about the experience afterwards, and Howell's account appeared in the *Journal of the American Medical Association*, May 19, 1975. In it, he noted that Lindbergh had planned his death as thoroughly as he had planned his trip across the Atlantic. Son Land Lindbergh told Jim Newton of the last days:

> He wasn't giving up, he was accepting, rising to the challenge. If it was inevitable, he wanted to prepare for the inevitable. He felt, "I can do something about this. The doctors have had their chance, and now it's my go." This, I think, gave him a tremendous amount of strength.

When they arrived at the Maui cottage, Land continued:

> He thought it was just great, he'd made it, he could relax, he could breathe the air. He felt much better. He had his family with him. The whole New York hospital atmosphere disappeared. All the machines and the tubes and the shots—had just gone. His appetite improved tremendously.

Round-the-clock care was provided by the family and two nurses—Rosemary Howell, the physician's daughter-in-law, and Mrs. Don Julian, the wife of Howell's relief doctor. Through the week, quasi-military planning sessions were held bedside, the commanding officer in full charge. Tevi Kahaleuahi brought progress reports on the grave preparation. The general had designed it. It was to be twelve feet deep, complete with a plan for drainage. Tevi had to dig with a back hoe down through lava rock. Scott and Land joined neighbor workmen on the hand digging. Ranch boss Hanchett regularly reported on the construction of the coffin, which the patient had asked to be made of locally grown hardwood. The foreman had assigned his cowboys to build it of eucalyptus, and it was heavy. He wanted to be buried with a Hudson's Bay blanket he had once brought from Canada for his mother. Land's wife, Susie Lindbergh, sent it in time from Montana.

Lindbergh asked Howell to spread the word that people should wear their work clothes to the funeral and not get dressed up. The doctor objected:

> These people wouldn't go to anybody's funeral without cleaning up and putting on their best clothes, their brother's or anybody's. You shouldn't dictate to them what they should wear to your funeral. You should let them express themselves in this way if they want to.

And they did.

In planning with Charles for the funeral service, Roselle Howell and Anne Lindbergh had tried out a few hymns often sung in Hawaiian churches. He was unenthusiastic, joshing Anne about her singing and calling some of the songs "corny." As a way around it, they sang them in Hawaiian.

On Monday morning, August 26, 1974, death came to Charles A. Lindbergh. He was seventy-two. As he had requested, he was buried within hours. Dying at 7:00 a.m., he was buried at 2:00 p.m. He wanted to be laid away in his work clothes—no embalming, no buttons or belt buckles, nothing that would not become, along with his body, a part of the earth. Some suspected the haste was to insure getting into the ground before the news people could arrive. His doctor denies this. The law required that an unembalmed body must be buried within eight hours.

It was Tevi who lifted the long frame from the bed in the cottage and laid it lovingly in the coffin. The cowboys loaded the cargo onto the back of Babes Hanchett's pickup truck. Tevi stood barefoot in the back, tying down a tarpaulin. It was a simple procession—the pickup, a jeep, the doctor's car, a nurse, and a policeman. As it went over the bridge at the Seven Pools, the tourists had no idea what it was.

The family asked Howell to take charge overall and be their spokesman with the press. He arranged for a sergeant from the county police, David J. K. Marciel, to patrol the churchyard. The officer thought his orders were to keep everybody out, and so he did. Howell later said no one had a right to do that, but it was done. Marciel, who was to devote his police career to youth drug prevention, stood guard that day at the top of the church road. He had come to know Lindbergh six months earlier, when the latter came to renew his driver's license at police headquarters in Wailuku, the county seat. "We talked airplanes for a half hour," he said. "That man was still checked out to fly 707s, at his age."

Three journalists had heard Lindbergh was dying and chartered a plane for the thirty-minute air trip from Honolulu to Hana and a car to cover the forty-five minutes of rough road from Hana to Kipahulu. They were Ron Edmonds, Associated Press photographer; Dan Carmichael, United Press International; and Pierre Bowman, *Honolulu Star-Bulletin*. Edmonds eight years later was to receive a Pulitzer Prize for his news picture of President Reagan being shot. Impressed with the sergeant's tight lid, the photographer whispered to his colleagues to engage the officer in conversation while he sneaked along the hedge to the church on the other side of the pasture. In a few moments Marciel, without taking his eyes off the remaining two, said, "You tell your friend that if he crosses that field, I'm gonna shoot him." They persuaded Edmonds to return. The officer admitted later he had no such authority and could not have made good on the threat. UPI's Dan Carmichael hid in the bushes before the service. Anne said it was all right for him to stay, as long as there were no interviews or pictures. His were the words that took the story to the world. Some media people arrived late, and Dr. Howell invited all to meet with him in the afternoon on the lawn of his home a few miles away to answer their questions.

Two services were held in the Palapala Ho'omau church: the burial service on Monday, August 26, and a memorial service the following day, held chiefly because people like Jon Lindbergh and Sam Pryor were unable to be present for the first one. Those who attended the Monday service recall how Helen Pahuwai, a Hawaiian lady who knew the Lindberghs, arose spontaneously from her seat, walked forward barefoot, and in the Hawaiian tradition emptied her apronful of hibiscus and plumeria blossoms onto the casket. Both services were coconducted by Henry Kahula, Hawaiian service-station manager and lay minister, and the Rev. Mr. Tincher, temporarily the pastor of Hana's Wananalua Congregational, the mother church of Palapala Ho'omau. Tincher's words appeared in newspapers worldwide.

> We commit the body of Charles A. Lindbergh to its final resting place, but his spirit we commend to Almighty God, knowing that death is but a new adventure in existence and remembering how Jesus said upon the cross, "Into thy hands I commend my spirit."

For the Tuesday service, Anne, at Dr. Howell's suggestion, invited the newspeople who were standing outside to come in and take seats. In view of the family's long-standing media problems, it was a gentle gesture of healing. This ceremony was a longer one and, in addition to Hebrew and Christian scriptures, included readings that Charles had chosen from Saint Augustine, Mahatma Gandhi, Hindu writings, a Hawaiian poem, and a Navajo prayer. A quartet closed the service with one of the Islands' great favorites, *O Kou Aloha No,* "The Queen's Prayer," composed by Hawaii's last reigning monarch, Queen Liliuokalani.

The *Honolulu Star-Bulletin* headlined Pierre Bowman's account:

EAGLE'S FINAL FLIGHT IN PRIVACY

Bowman covered both services, calling them "incredible." He was one of the reporters who was highly critical of the way the press had treated the "eagle" and was quietly moved "to think that this person could end in such simplicity and dignity."

The remains lie in a simple grave a few yards from a cliff that plunges 180 feet straight down to the crashing sea. The immediate grave area is built up to a level slightly above the ground, in the Hawaiian custom, and is covered with black lava *'ili'ili* stones, smoothed by the longtime pounding of the surf below. The grave is set off by a low-lying pinioned chain, a gift from the pilot's early flying friend, Bud Gurney.

At first there was a crush of visitors with great numbers of automobiles lined up on the road. Naturally, with such crowds, some of the etiquette was not of the best. Neighbors became alarmed, and Anne received disturbing reports about graveyard conduct.

Church officials invited her to draft some appropriate language which they then mounted on the grounds:

> You are welcome to enter this church in a spirit of reverence befitting any place of worship. Those who wish to walk quietly on the surrounding paths are asked not to step on the graves or disturb stones or flowers, out of respect for the deceased and consideration for the feelings of the relatives.

In recent years the numbers of callers have notably subsided, and the deportment is respectful. People speak of the serenity there.

The simple granite stone was designed by Charles and Anne:

CHARLES A. LINDBERGH

Born Michigan 1902   Died Maui 1974

If I take the wings of the morning and
dwell in the uttermost parts of the sea

C.A.L.

There are visitors who are surprised to see the position of the initials. Did someone think Lindbergh was the author of the lines from Scripture? The official explanation is that the space at the left was for "A.M.L.," in case Anne was also to be buried there. In Hawaii it would be inauspicious to inscribe her initials in advance.

Sam Pryor thought people should know the context of the quotation on the stone and would frequently read to graveside visitors the portion of the 139th Psalm where the lines are found:

Whither shall I go from thy spirit? or
Whither shall I flee from thy presence?
If I ascend up into heaven, thou art there;
If I make my bed in hell, behold, thou art there.
If I take the wings of the morning,
And dwell in the uttermost parts of the sea,
Even there shall thy hand lead me,
And thy right hand shall hold me.

Some neighbors have questioned the decision to locate a world hero's grave in a previously undisturbed setting, inevitably to be disturbed by both the curious and the respectful. Lindbergh had been on hand for the cremations of his father, a sister, and a son. Why would he not have chosen this route, the ashes distributed over the waves he had transcended? The answer may lie in his wish to have a completely earthy death and burial, and a desire to be a part of the natural decomposition process, which he saw as an integral part of life.

My aging body transmits an ageless life stream. Molecular and
atomic replacement change life's composition. After my death,
the molecules of my being will return to the earth and the sky.
They came from the stars. I am of the stars.

20

Epilogue

Future generations may appreciate Charles A. Lindbergh better than do contemporary ones. Mention his name today, and the response is more likely to be a criticism arising from some controversy than an awareness of his productive legacies. But history has its own way with such things. He will, of course, be forever known for his pioneering in the air. He will also be remembered by some for his landmark contributions to surgery, rocketry, literature, and the effort to balance technology and the natural environment.

Yet beyond these images, Lindbergh may already have emerged posthumously as a seer, a thesis advanced by Theodore I. Malinin, Miami research surgeon, biographer of Alexis Carrel, and the aviator's latter-day colleague on the perfusion heart pump. It is quite possible that in addition to his highly visible material and physical accomplishments, Charles A. Lindbergh will also be appreciated for his battle for the world's soul—especially because of his devotion to the quality of the earth and the quality of the spirit.

In September 1973, the old warrior paid a final visit to his boyhood home in Minnesota. He was seventy-one and his illness was beginning to show gaunt in his face. Within a year he would be gone. He was in Little Falls to speak at the dedication of the Lindbergh Interpretive Center, a neat, modern mini-museum in the woods, presenting in display graphics the story of the family heritage and of his life.

Of the homes he most cherished across the globe, including those on the islands of Illiec on the Atlantic and Maui in the Pacific, he wrote, "The old farm at Little Falls is the only other place I have loved as much." On this final visit, he roamed through the woods that had been a pasture when as a teenager he had run the farm for two years. He saw again the spot where he had picked up an Indian spearhead. He was pleased that the small pond he had made for watering his ducks, using his own experimental concrete mix, was still showing nary a crack after fifty-four Minnesota winters. He checked out the riverbank where he and his friends used to swim, and paused again at the screened porch on the river side of the house, where he slept out both summer and winter. He recalled the stories his father told him about his, C. A.'s, boyhood farm, thirty-five miles to the southwest, and their family's episodes with neighboring Chippewa and Sioux.

Characteristically, the homecomer had carefully worked out what he wanted to say to his listeners at the dedication. The remarks suggest he was also speaking, once again with the long view, to a wider audience. He had shown the prepared text to his friend Russell Fridley, director of the Minnesota Historical Society, who urged him to lengthen his material for such a significant occasion. But the speaker declined and held to seven minutes.

From the steps of the old farm house, Charles Lindbergh shared moving reflections about happy years in the unspoiled outdoors. He had seen frontier history made on the Mississippi, flowing near where he was standing—Indians in their canoes, trappers, hunters, and loggers. Yet the river had spoken to him not only of the past; it had also signaled for him the future. He described the first biplane he had ever seen or heard, roaring up the valley and calling him to new worlds. Later it was possible for people from the riverbank at night to watch "a satellite penetrate through the stars." Yet he believed "our civilization's latest advance is symbolized by the park rather than by satellites and space travel." In establishing parks and nature reserves, he said, people reach "beyond the material values of science and technology" to "the miraculous spiritual awareness that only nature in balance can maintain."

As our civilization advances, if our follies permit it to advance, I feel sure we will realize that progress can be measured only by the quality of life—all life, not human life alone. The accumulation of knowledge, the discoveries of science, the products of technology, our ideals, our art, our social structures, all the achievements of mankind have value only to the extent that they preserve and improve the quality of life.

As he said, Charles Lindbergh came from the earth and the stars. He has returned to the earth and the stars. Whoever is behind the stars enriched our lives by sending this one among us. To the best of his lights he did what he could to preserve and improve the quality of life.

He asks us to do the same.

Appendix A: Great in Character

These words are excerpted from a tribute written in Kipahulu at the time of Lindbergh's death. It was entitled "Shadows and Lights" and dated August 1974. The author is unknown.

One of those few in history to achieve the heights of worldwide fame, for the past three decades he had sought the shadows of anonymity, giving freely of his time to the cause of conservation, as well as to the sharing of his wealth of technical knowledge in the field of aviation.

The "Lone Eagle" they called him when he was twenty-five years old, and the "Lone Eagle" he remained until his death at seventy-two. Charles Lindbergh achieved success in many areas of endeavor, but such deeds tend to fade into the academic obscurity of a history book. It was for his greatness of character that he was and will always be a Living Legend. For all the fame and fortune, which came overnight to a very young man, he remained modest, self-effacing, and austere in his lifestyle, giving of himself all his days.

And now he has left this world in the same way he lived—from a simple stone cottage to an almost hidden graveyard deep in the jungle-like foliage of eastern Maui. Of all the places in the world he had visited, and there were few he missed, he loved best the beauty and simplicity of the Hana coast. He chose the ancient burial ground deep in the shade of a towering banyan tree—the same as he had chosen the shadow of anonymity in life. That small corner of hallowed land will become a shrine for people of all time to a man great in character as well as in deed.

Thomas Paine once said, "Reputation is what men and women think of us: character is what God and the angels know of us." If this is true, Charles Lindbergh will find his path ahead bathed in the true light of glory—a brightness from which he will feel no need to hide.

Appendix B: The Aloha Cottage

The Hawaiian word Aloha, *love, has many expressions, including welcome and farewell. Lindbergh's* Aloha *to his friends and family was said in a cottage overlooking the sea with the surf pounding on the huge lava rocks below. This charming guest cabin was turned over to the Lindbergh family by Ed and Jeannie Pechin for the final eight days. A month later, September 22, 1974, Anne wrote from her home in Connecticut in appreciation for their care.*

Dear Mr. & Mrs. Pechin,

You must be back in Hana looking at that beautiful coastline that is now engraved in my mind from our week there. I wish there were some way of my telling you what your generosity in letting us use your guest cottage meant to my husband, to the boys, and to me and to every one in my family—even those who were not there—who have shared with us by letter or by talk the experience of that week before my husband died. To my husband it meant carrying out his last wish, to go home to Maui. To us, my sons and me, who were privileged to share it with him, it meant a chance for an intimacy in his life, his thoughts, his feelings, we never could have had if he had been in the hospital.

I hope you do not feel that the beautiful cottage is marked with tragedy because of this experience. Of course it is deep sadness to lose a husband or a father. But for him it was a kind of triumph. He was so happy and at peace to be there, to hear the waves and the birds and to have his family about him. For us it will always be one of the richest and deepest experiences of our lives. I feel this kind of blessing will go down through the families of all our children into the lives of the grandchildren, who will be stronger to face life and death because of it.

I am grateful to all of Hana and Kipahulu, all of Maui in a sense, for the outpouring of love, and help, and sympathy that surrounded us there. But the core of it seems to me to be expressed in that beautiful little cottage and your kindness in letting us use it. I am now back in a world very different from Hana, in the rush and pressure of many duties and demands and the complications of settling an estate and of finding a

147

new life lived alone. But I hope when things are in somewhat better order, I can find something from our life together—Charles's and my lives—that can go to your life there, as a more personal and tangible expression of our gratitude. I think our last meeting was at the David Grays' porch in Kipahulu. I will look forward to meeting you again when I return to Maui, I hope this winter sometime. With my warmest wishes for you and deep gratitude for you,

s/ Anne Lindbergh

Appendix C: The Lindbergh Miracle

The most perceptive contemporary comment on the trans-Atlantic flight and the man who made it was offered by Frederick Lewis Allen, long time editor of Harper's *magazine, in his historical and sociological review of the 1920s,* Only Yesterday.

The owner of the Brevoort and Lafayette Hotels in New York, Raymond Orteig, had offered—way back in 1919—a prize of $25,000 for the first non-stop flight between New York and Paris. Only a few days after the conclusion of the Snyder-Gray trial, three planes were waiting for favorable weather conditions to hop off from Roosevelt Field, just outside New York, in quest of this prize: The *Columbia,* which was to be piloted by Clarence Chamberlin and Lloyd Bertaud; the *America,* with Lieutenant-Commander Byrd of North Pole fame in command; and the *Spirit of St. Louis,* which had abruptly arrived from the Pacific coast with a lone young man named Charles A. Lindbergh at the controls. There was no telling which of the three planes would get off first, but clearly the public favorite was the young man from the West. He was modest, he seemed to know his business, there was something particularly daring about his idea of making the perilous journey alone, and he was as attractive-looking a youngster as ever had faced a camera man. The reporters—to his annoyance—called him "Lucky Lindy" and the "Flying Fool." The spotlight of publicity was upon him. Not yet, however, was he a god.

On the evening of May 19, 1927, Lindbergh decided that although it was drizzling on Long Island, the weather reports gave a chance of fair skies for his trip and he had better get ready. He spent the small hours of the next morning in sleepless preparations, went to Curtiss Field, received further weather news, had his plane trundled to Roosevelt Field and fueled, and a little before eight o'clock—on the morning of May 20th—climbed in and took off for Paris.

Then something very like a miracle took place.

No sooner had the word been flashed along the wires that Lindbergh had started than the whole population of the country became united in the exaltation of a common emotion. Young and old, rich and poor, farmer and stockbroker, Fundamentalist and skeptic, highbrow and lowbrow, all with one accord fastened their hopes upon the young man in the *Spirit of St. Louis*. To give a single instance of the intensity of their mood: at the Yankee Stadium in New York, where the Maloney-Sharkey fight was held on the evening of the 20th, forty thousand hard-boiled boxing fans rose as one man and stood with bared heads in impressive silence when the announcer asked them to pray for Lindbergh. The next day came the successive reports of Lindbergh's success—he had reached the Irish coast, he was crossing over England, he was over the Channel, he had landed at Le Bourget to be enthusiastically mobbed by a vast crowd of Frenchmen—and the American people went almost mad with joy and relief. And when the reports of Lindbergh's first few days in Paris showed that he was behaving with charming modesty and courtesy, millions of his countrymen took him to their hearts as they had taken no other human being in living memory.

Every record for mass excitement and mass enthusiasm in the age of ballyhoo was smashed during the next few weeks. Nothing seemed to matter, either to the newspapers or to the people who read them, but Lindbergh and his story. On the day the flight was completed the *Washington Star* sold 16,000 extra copies, the *St. Louis Post-Dispatch* 40,000, the *New York Evening World* 114,000. The huge headlines which described Lindbergh's triumphal progress from day to day in newspapers from Maine to Oregon showed how thorough was public agreement with the somewhat extravagant dictum of the *Evening World* that Lindbergh had performed "the greatest feat of a solitary man in the records of the human race." Upon his return to the United States, a single Sunday issue of a single paper contained one hundred columns of text and pictures devoted to him. Nobody appeared to question the fitness of President Coolidge's action in sending a cruiser of the United States navy to bring this young citizen and his plane back from France. He was greeted in Washington at a vast open-air gathering at which the President made—according to Charles Merz—"the longest and most impressive address since his annual message to Congress." The Western Union having provided form messages for telegrams of congratulations to Lindbergh on his arrival, 55,000 of them were sent to him—and were loaded on a truck and trundled after him in the parade through Washington. One telegram, from Minneapolis, was signed with 17,500 names and made up a scroll 520 feet long, under which ten messenger boys staggered. After the public welcome in New York, the Street Cleaning Department gathered up 1,800 tons of paper which had been torn up and thrown out of windows of office buildings to make a snowstorm of greeting—1,800 tons as against a mere 155 tons swept up after the premature Armistice celebration of November 7, 1918!

Lindbergh was commissioned Colonel, and received the Distinguished Flying Cross, the Congressional Medal of Honor, and so many foreign decorations and honorary memberships that to repeat the list would be a weary task. He was offered two and a half million dollars for a tour of the world by air, and $700,000 to appear in the films; his signature was sold for $1,600; a Texas town was named for him, a thirteen-hundred-foot Lindbergh tower was proposed for the city of Chicago, "the largest dinner ever tendered to an individual in modern history" was consumed in his honor, and a staggering number of streets, schools, restaurants, and corporations sought to share the glory of his name.

Nor was there any noticeable group of dissenters from all this hullabaloo. Whatever else people might disagree about, they joined in praise of him.

To appreciate how extraordinary was this universal outpouring of admiration and love—for the word love is hardly too strong—one must remind oneself of two or three facts.

Lindbergh's flight was not the first crossing of the Atlantic by air. Alcock and Brown had flown direct from Newfoundland to Ireland in 1919. That same year the N-C4, with five men aboard, had crossed by way of the Azores, and the British dirigible R-34 had flown from Scotland to Long Island with 31 men aboard, and then had turned about and made a return flight to England. The German dirigible ZR-3 (later known as the *Los Angeles* had flown from Friedrichshafen to Lakehurst, New Jersey, in 1924 with 32 people aboard. Two Round-the-World American army planes had crossed the North Atlantic by way of Iceland, Greenland, and Newfoundland in 1924. The novelty of Lindbergh's flight lay only in the fact that he went all the way from New York to Paris instead of jumping off from Newfoundland, that he reached his precise objective, and that he went alone.

Furthermore, there was little practical advantage in such an exploit. It brought about a boom in aviation, to be sure, but a not altogether healthy one, and it led many a flyer to hop off blindly for foreign shores in emulation of Lindbergh and be drowned. Looking back on the event after a lapse of years, and stripping it of its emotional connotations, one sees it simply as a daring stunt flight—the longest up to that time. Why, then, this idolization of Lindbergh?

The explanation is simple. A disillusioned nation fed on cheap heroics and scandal and crime was revolting against the low estimate of human nature which it had allowed itself to entertain. For years the American people had been spiritually starved. They had seen their early ideals and illusions and hopes one by one worn away by the corrosive influence of events and ideas—by the disappointing aftermath of the war, by scientific doctrines and psychological theories which undermined their religion and ridiculed their sentimental notions, by the spectacle of graft in politics and crime on the city streets, and finally by their recent newspaper diet of smut and murder. Romance, chivalry, and self-dedication had been debunked; the heroes of history had been revealed as people with queer complexes. There was the god of business to worship—but a suspicion lingered that he was made of brass. Ballyhoo had given the public contemporary heroes to bow down before—but these contemporary heroes, with their fat profits from moving-picture contracts and ghost-written syndicated articles, were not wholly convincing. Something that people needed, if they were to live at peace with themselves and with the world, was missing from their lives. And all at once Lindbergh provided it. Romance, chivalry, self-dedication—here they were, embodied in a modern Galahad for a generation which had foresworn Galahads. Lindbergh did not accept the moving-picture offers that came his way, he did not sell testimonials, did not boast, did not get himself involved in scandal, conducted himself with unerring taste—and was handsome and brave withal. The machinery of ballyhoo was ready and waiting to lift him up where every eye could see him. Is it any wonder that the public's reception of him took on the aspects of a vast religious revival?

Lindbergh did not go back on his admirers. He undertook a series of exhibition flights and good-will flights—successfully and with quiet dignity. He married a daughter of the ambassador to Mexico, and in so doing delighted the country by turning the tables on ballyhoo itself—by slipping away with his bride on a motor-boat and remaining hidden for days despite the efforts of hundreds of newspaper men to spy upon his honeymoon. Wherever he went, crowds fought for a chance to be near him, medals were pinned upon him, tributes were showered upon him, his coming and going was news. He packed away a good-sized fortune earned chiefly as consultant for aviation companies, but few people grudged him that. Incredibly, he kept his head and his instinct for fine conduct.

And he remained a national idol.

Even three and four years after his flight, the roads about his New Jersey farm were blocked on week-ends with the cars of admirers who wanted to catch a glimpse of him, and it was said that he could not even send his shirts to a laundry because they did not come back—they were too valuable as souvenirs. His picture hung in hundreds of schoolrooms and in thousands of houses. No living American—no dead American, one might almost say, save perhaps Abraham Lincoln—commanded such unswerving fealty. You might criticize Coolidge or Hoover or Ford or Edison or Bobby Jones or any other headline hero; but if you decried anything that Lindbergh did, you knew that you had wounded your auditors. For Lindbergh was a god.

Pretty good, one reflects, for a stunt flyer. But also, one must add, pretty good for the American people. They had shown that they had better taste in heroes than anyone would have dared to predict during the years which immediately preceded the 20th of May, 1927.

Appendix D: Farewell Address

In September 1973 Charles Lindbergh returned for the last time to his boyhood home in Little Falls, Minnesota, to dedicate the new Lindbergh Interpretive Center. His remarks, reprinted in part here, eloquently expressed his love for the site and his concern for humanity's future.

To me, this park brings contact with a great span of American history. I think of the centuries that the river beside us carried a traffic of Indian canoes. At one time or another, tepees must have been pitched on every flat area of the valley. Surely hunters with their bows and arrows killed game where we are assembled now. Not far from here, when I was a boy, I found a carnelian spearhead.

Early trappers carried their furs down this river, and I myself remember the wanigans and bateaux of the lumber companies. It is now hard to visualize the big log jams that were once held by the river's rocks and shoals. My father and I often walked out over them and swam at their outer edges.

I can even connect the Mississippi here with aviation. One day, before the first World War began, when I was playing upstairs in our house, I heard an unusually loud engine noise. I ran to the window and climbed out onto the roof. There was an airplane flying upriver, below the treetops on the banks. I learned that it was carrying passengers from a field near Little Falls. Of course I wanted to fly in it, but my mother said that would be much too expensive and dangerous.

I might end by saying that on this riverbank one can look upward in late evening and watch a satellite penetrate through stars, thereby spanning human progress from the primitive hunter with his canoe to the latest advance of our civilization. But in saying so, I would be stopping short of our latest advance. I believe our civilization's latest advance is symbolized by the park rather than by satellites and space travel. In establishing parks and nature reserves, man reaches beyond the material values of science and technology. He recognizes the essential value of life itself, of life's natural inheritance irreplaceably evolved through earthly epochs, of the miraculous spiritual awareness that only nature in balance can maintain.

As our civilization advances, if our follies permit it to advance, I feel sure we will realize that progress can be measured only by the quality of life—all life, not human life alone. The accumulation of knowledge, the discoveries of science, the products of technology, our ideals, our art, our social structures—all the achievements of mankind—have value only to the extent that they preserve and improve the quality of life.

This is why I say that parks symbolize the greatest advance our civilization has yet made.

Appendix E: Selected Words

Charles Lindbergh wrote and published seven books. In them he felt free to express his deepest thoughts. Here are some.

Balance

The survival of our civilization depends upon its quality, and its quality depends in turn upon its balance—a balance which is being destroyed by the excesses of science. . . . Science is upsetting this balance with an overemphasis of mind and a neglect of spirit and body. To survive, we must keep the balance. To progress, we must improve it.

Bible

[In youth] As I lost confidence in the Bible, I gained confidence in science.

[Preparing for 1944 service in South Pacific] Purchased a small New Testament. Since I can carry only one book— and a very small one—that is my choice. It would not have been a decade ago; but the more I learn and the more I read, the less competition it has.

Body

Why should I concern myself with engine failure? . . . The explosion of the engine will be inseparable from the beat of my heart. As I trust one, I'll trust the other.

Fatigue never does catch up with you if the goal you have is great enough.

Character

With every day that passes, I realize more fully that, aside from a plane with performance enough to make the flight, my greatest asset lies in the character of my partners in Saint Louis.

The efficiency of a factory is less important than the character it builds in its workers and the effect of its product on our nation.

Our short term survival may depend on the knowledge of atomic scientists and the performance of super-sonic aircraft. Our long term survival depends, alone, on the character of man.

Church

Notre Dame and Sainte-Chapelle are beautiful but somewhat spoiled by the tourist atmosphere. I have no feeling of religion in these places. The only time I have sensed religion in one of these old places was at Mont-Saint-Michel, when Anne and I were alone in the moonlight late at night. Places of religion should not be thrown open to tourists, except, possibly, at times which are especially set aside. . . . Better to spend an hour in Notre Dame, and the rest of the day thinking about it. That would leave a worthwhile and permanent impression on your memory.

Christ

We are children of marriages,
      influenced by the culture of Greece,
      guided by the sermons of Christ,
      inspired by the death of martyrs,
      instructed by western knowledge,
      protected by western arms.

From the spirit of Christ,
from the mind of science,
from the bodily inheritance of farmers and pioneers—
from such elements, western people have achieved a balance unequalled by any civilization of the past.

Christmas

It seems to me that Christmas has deviated as much from the birth of Christ as Christianity has from his teachings. The keynote at the birth of Christ was simplicity. The keynote of Christmas today is luxury. The birth and life of Christ were surrounded by things mystical. Christmas and Christianity today are surrounded with things material. I would like to have a simple, uncluttered, silent Christmas. Christmas should be a day that brings one closer to God and to the philosophy of Christ.

Anne has made a very simple and beautiful little creche in the library, and we had music and reading in front of it, with the children taking part. . . . It was the best Christmas Eve we have ever had.

Danger

Carrel once said that some contact with danger was essential to the building of character in children, and I believe this is correct. Life can be made so precious that it is not worth living.

The way to meet danger is to move toward it.

What justifies the risk of life? Some answer, the attainment of knowledge. Some say wealth, or power, is sufficient cause. I believe the risks I take are justified by the sheer love of the life I lead.

Death

[About aerial combat] There was freedom even in the duel of life and death—his bullets and my bullets—the freedom of life if they passed, the freedom of death if they struck.

Devil

God must let the devil have his way with men. Is that being absolutely loving? If the good comes from God, and the bad comes from the devil— when you have two opposites like that—there must be some relative ground between them. You can't expect people to be all good. . . . Personally, I don't think God wants me to lose all contact with the devil.

Democracy

We Americans are a primitive people. We do not have discipline. Our moral standards are low. . . . It shows in the newspapers, the morbid curiosity over crimes and murder trials. Americans seem to have little respect for law, or the rights of others. . . . The English have greater regard for law and order than the people of any other nation.

If we succeed, it will be less by forcing our system of democracy on others than by setting an example others wish to follow; less by using arms than by avoiding them; less by pointing out the "mote" in another's eye than by removal of the "beam" in our own. The improvement of our way of life is more important than the spreading of it.

Family

Anne is wonderful with her children. I have never known anyone who I think understands children as well. They cannot help developing character with such a mother.

Force

It seems that a treaty, to be effective, must be backed by strength—just as a law, to be effective, must be backed by a police force.

[Declining a white hunter's invitation to help kill a rhinoceros that had gored an African man] I've changed my mind. It would just be an eye for an eye and a tooth for a tooth, and I gave that up after World War II.

God

When we worship God and live by His spiritual values, the knowledge and infinite complexity of science are channeled by a wisdom beyond human capability. . . . Science intensifies religious truth by cleansing it of ignorance and superstition. Then science gives us the material strength to protect our spiritual values.

I now realize that while God cannot be seen as tangibly as I had demanded as a child, His presence can be sensed in every sight and act and incident. I know that when one loses this sense, he misses the true quality of life. He loses the infinite strength without which no people can survive.

Scientific man has enthroned knowledge as his idol, and turned his back on God.

Knowledge

Perhaps there was a wisdom in the old myth of the Garden of Eden. "But of the tree of knowledge. . . . thou shalt not eat of it; for in the day that thou eatest thereof thou shalt surely die." In this early record, both man's fascination and his fear of knowledge are recorded. That he must search for it was accepted. That it involved great danger for him was already understood.

Materialism

We will always be on the defensive unless we commit ourselves to vigorous and positive moral policies. We need to reach beyond materialism to a philosophy springing from the character of man and the truths of God.

These thoughts represent a journey from my early confidence in the limitless future of scientific man, to an apprehension of the crisis to which a scientific materialism has led him.

We must discard the materialistic philosophy that the end justifies the means. Means and ends are inseparable.

Mysticism

Biological studies and experiments had increased my basic interest in fields of mysticism. The experience of war intensified this interest. I came to the conclusion that life's greatest values did not lie in results to be obtained through biological mechanics.

Carrel believes in a mysticism that extended apart from and beyond science. He was fascinated by the overlapping peripheries of mystical and scientific worlds. That fascination corresponded with and intensified my own.

[Watching Carrel perform an operation] I felt I had reached the frontier where the mystical and the scientific meet, where I would see across the indistinct borders separating life from death. When I donned my gown, I prepared for a supernatural experience. Then what was life? And what was death? Did nothing mystical exist beyond cellular relationships, no greater God than beings rounded out with flesh?

I talked with Sir Francis Younghusband, the famed explorer and mystic, who did not believe the mechanics of life were of prime importance. . . . I outlined my interest in physical bridges across which man might pass between the continents of science and mysticism, flesh and spirit.

Nazism

I was stirred by the spirit in Germany as I had been deadened by the lack of it in England and disturbed by its volatile individuality in France. But for me the ideology, the regimentation, the intolerance, and the fanaticism of Hitler's Third Reich were intolerable in comparison to alternatives that existed.

Prayer

We must draw strength from the forgotten virtues of simplicity, humility, contemplation, and prayer. It requires a dedication beyond science, beyond self, but the rewards are great, and it is our only hope.

Press

I suppose if I had any resentment in my life, it would be against the press. I know they're paid to get pictures and stories. It's their job. But there's a place for humanity. Don't think I don't appreciate [reported reconciliations between labor and management]. But it would be quite something else for me to go to a newspaper editor or publisher and say, "I'm sorry for being resentful for the way your people have treated me and my family." In the first place, they'd just laugh at me. And, more important, do you think it would change the way the press behaves? Maybe I enjoy having a resentment or two. They're like pepper. They keep life sharp and interesting. Without them life would be too bland.

Pride
Our sense of superiority over other creatures, and our pride in our mastery of the Earth need the humbling perspective that the wildness of nature brings to us.

Progress
If we are to lead mankind through these black years, if we are to be successful in war and peace, we must have clearly in mind what we desire in civilization and what constitutes human progress.

Quality of Life
The quality of life is more important than life itself.

Our security, our freedom, our democratic system itself depends on maintaining an extraordinary quality in our people.

This altitude flight at Willow Run [where he self-tested pilot body response in the upper atmosphere] taught me that in worshiping science man gains power but loses the quality of life.

Perhaps survival, in the last analysis, was fully as dependent on the quality of life as on the power of arms—dependent on a perpetual balance of spiritual and material forces.

Rationality
> The longer I live, the more limited I believe rationality to be. I have found that the irrational gives man insight he cannot otherwise attain.

Religion
> *[Letter to Henry Ford]* You combine the characteristics that I admire most in men—success with humility, firmness with tolerance, science with religion. I shall not attempt to make a longer list.

Risk
> I do not believe in taking foolish chances. But nothing can be accomplished without taking any chance at all.

Salvation
> We must realize that salvation lies first within us—and only secondarily in our governments, treaties, and laws.

> There is no materialistic solution, no political formula, which alone can save us. Our salvation, and our only salvation, lies in controlling the arm of western science by the mind of a Western philosophy guided by the eternal truths of God.

Science
> Why work for the idol of science when it demands the sacrifice of cities full of children: when it makes robots out of people and blinds their eyes to God?

> We are in the grip of a scientific materialism, caught in the vicious cycle where our security today seems to depend on regimentation and weapons which will ruin us tomorrow.

> To me in youth, science was more important than either man or God. The one I took for granted; the other was too intangible for me to understand. Like most modern youth, I worshiped science. I was awed by its knowledge.

Now I have lived to experience the early results of scientific materialism. I have seen the science I worshiped, and the aircraft I loved, destroying the civilization I expected them to serve.

If we are to keep science from destroying that part of our civilization which is left, if it is to be the great benefit to mankind that we have hoped, we must control it by a philosophy reaching beyond materialism, a philosophy rooted in the character of man and nourished by the eternal truths of God.

The tragedy of scientific man is that he has found no way to guide his own discoveries to a constructive end.

With the key of science, man has turned loose forces which he cannot re-imprison.

A few hours before, I would have viewed the Willow Run bomber production line as a marvelous feat of engineering. I would have felt proud of even the small part I had in bringing it into being. Now, it seemed a terrible giant's womb, growling, clanging, giving birth to robots which were killing people by the thousands each day as they destroyed the culture of Europe. . . . This was a temple of the god of science at which we moderns worshiped. . . . Here I watched a steel door lift and an airplane roll outside; while, in reality, the walls of a cathedral fell and children died.

Somehow man must be made to see that science was hypnotizing him with its machines, dulling his senses with its knowledge, destroying his culture with its bombs.

How could we further human progress by striving for such scientific goals [building planes to fly higher and faster] when the very concentration on them blinded us to higher values, mocked the brotherhood of man, shielded us from God?

Here in [postwar] Germany, the truths of science and the truths of religion had clashed, and religion remained to teach its ancient lesson. It was true that modern civilization could not live without science, as I discovered in the South Pacific. It was also true that science alone lacked the wisdom needed to survive.

The intellectual truths of great scientists are being perverted by the material exploitation of industry and war. Hiroshima was as far from the intention of the pure scientist as the Inquisition was from the Sermon on the Mount.

Was there something inherently self-destroying in the worship of science? Was science's power of survival only temporary, capable of winning battles but not of saving man? Was there something even inherently dangerous in the unguided search for knowledge?

In their search for materialistic power, the Germans had set up science as their God, and science had destroyed them.

If we are to control the science we have created, if we are to lead the peoples of the world to a better future, we must first search our own souls.

Speeches

There is something clean and sharp and right about addressing a meeting. But one of these "buffet suppers" or "cocktail parties" seems to be a kind of prostitution of human effort. . . . If it weren't for the intensity of my feeling about this war, no amount of money, or persuasion, or anything else, could get me to attend such things.

If and when this war ends, I hope I never have to make speeches again.

Standards

Our standards must be based on man himself, his relationship to God and to his fellow-men.

Accuracy means something to me. It's vital to my sense of values. I've learned not to trust people who are inaccurate. Every aviator knows that if mechanics are inaccurate, aircraft crash. If pilots are inaccurate, they get lost—sometimes killed. In my profession, life itself depends on accuracy.

Truth

There was truth in the mathematics that designed a high-explosive bomb, in the machines that shaped the wings of a bomber, in the masses of data and cold logic which took man's minds from government and God until a Nazi party rose to shatter Europe. But it was truth unguided by moral principles; it was scientific truth, unbalanced by the truths of religion.

I now understand that spiritual truth is more essential to a nation than the mortar in its cities' walls. When the actions of a people are unguided by these truths, it is only a matter of time before their walls collapse.

War

[Noting atrocities committed by Americans in the Pacific] What is barbaric on one side of the earth is still barbaric on the other. "Judge not that ye be not judged." It is not the Germans alone, or the Japanese, but the men of all nations to whom this war has brought shame and degradation.

Bibliography

Allen, Frederick Lewis. *Only Yesterday*. New York: Harper & Brothers, 1931.

Fagan, George V. *The Air Force Academy*. Boulder: Johnson Books, 1988.

Gill, Brendan. *Lindbergh Alone*. New York: Harcourt Brace Jovanovich, 1977.

Larson, Bruce L. *Lindbergh of Minnesota* [Life of C. A.]. New York: Harcourt Brace Jovanovich, 1971.

Lindbergh, Anne Morrow. *North to the Orient*. New York: Harcourt, Brace and Company, 1935.

——. *Gift From The Sea*. New York: Random House, 1955.

——. *War Within and Without*. New York: Harcourt Brace Jovanovich, 1980.

Lindbergh, Charles A. *We*. New York: G. P. Putnam's Sons, 1927.

——. *The Culture of Organs* [with Alexis Carrel]. New York: P. B. Hoeber, 1938.

——. *Of Flight and Life*. New York: Charles Scribner's Sons, 1948.

——. *The Spirit of St. Louis*. New York: Charles Scribner's Sons, 1953.

——. *The Wartime Journals of Charles A. Lindbergh*. New York: Harcourt Brace Jovanovich, 1970.

——. *Boyhood on the Upper Mississippi*. Saint Paul: Minnesota Historical Society, 1972.

——. *Autobiography of Values*. New York: Harcourt Brace Jovanovich, 1977.

Mosley, Leonard. *Lindbergh: A Biography*. Garden City: Doubleday, 1976.

Newton, James D. *Uncommon Friends*. New York: Harcourt Brace Jovanovich, 1987.

Pryor, Samuel F., Jr. *All God's Creatures*. New York: Vantage Press, 1982.

Rogers, Will. *The Writings of Will Rogers*. (Daily Telegrams, Weekly Articles, Radio Broadcasts). Stillwater: Oklahoma State University Press, 1983.

Ross, Walter S. *The Last Hero*. New York: Harper & Row, 1964.

Smith, Truman. *Berlin Alert*. Stanford: Hoover Institution Press, 1984.

Index

Adams, James Luther 3
Adams, John 120
Adventures of Ideas 95
Air Force Academy 106
Air power 69, 111-12
Airmail controversy 70
Albatross 60
Alcoholics Anonymous 20n
Aldrin, Edwin "Buzz" 51
Allen, Frederick Lewis
   2, 35, 149
America First Committee
   74, 119
Andersen, Gov. Elmer L.
   xiii, 49, 93
Anti-Semitism 75
Apology 90, 119, 126
Armstrong, Neil 105
Army career 97
Arnold, Gen. Henry "Hap" 71
Atterbury, William W. 49
Autographs 56, 82

Berlin Alert 66
Bible 13, 45, 102, 139, 157
Bixby, Harold 34, 124
Bloom, Sol 110
Blythe, Dick 85
Bowman, Pierre 137
Brown, William Adams 45
Buchman, Frank N. D.
   20n, 64, 118
Burrage, Admiral Guy H. 43
Byrd, Admiral Richard E. 5

Carmichael, Daniel 136

Carrel, Alexis 17-19, 21, 24,
   91, 94, 141
Caterpillar Club 5
Character 7, 48, 105-06, 145
Church 13-14, 44, 125, 136-38
Churchill, Winston 64, 112
Cole, Wayne S. 112
Collins, Michael 51
Columbia Presb. Hospital 132
Concorde 107-08
Conservation 117
Coolidge, Calvin 37
"Copperhead" 72, 111
Culture of Organs, The 18
Curtiss "Jenny" 6

Darien, Connecticut 46
Death 31, 132-35
DeJetley, Tony and Alberta 126
Des Moines speech 73-75
Desert experience 28-29
Discipline, personal 47, 104
Doolittle, James 4

Earhart, Amelia 79
Early, Stephen T. 72, 92
Eisenhower, Dwight D. 98
Faith 15
Fear 30, 54
Fifth dimension 27-30
Firestone, Harvey 20
Fish, Hamilton 110
Ford, Henry 20, 115, 118
Forty-eight-state tour
   38-40, 103
Fredette, Col. Raymond 66
Fridley, Russell 49, 142

German people 63, 65, 77
Gift from the Sea 88, 124
God 12, 15, 21-23, 102,
    116, 137
Goddard, Robert H. 92, 105
Goering, Hermann 60
Gow, Betty 48
Gray, David 128
Great Awakening 120
Guggenheim, Carol 105, 119
Guggenheim Fund 38
Guggenheim, Harry 38-39
Guns 3, 97
Gurney, Harlan "Bud" 82, 138
Hana Maui Hotel 126
Hana Medical Center 133
Hanchett, Babes 135
Hanchett, John 124, 126, 135
Hasegawa General Store 126
Hasegawa, Harry 127
Hatred 70, 77
Hauptmann, Bruno 41-42
Hawaii Conference Foundation,
    UCC (Congregational) 125
Honesty 47-48, 107
Hoover, Herbert 38
Howell, Dr. Milton
    127, 133, 136
Howell, Roselle 128, 135
Howell, Rosemary 134
Human being, new type of 120
Human nature 25, 116, 120

Ickes, Harold L. 72, 92
Income tax 48

Jews, assistance to 60, 76
Jovanovich, William 133

Kahaleuahi, Joseph "Tevi"
    128, 135
Kahula, Henry 137
Keyhoe, Donald E. 39
Kipahulu Community
    Association 128
Konchellah, John Ole 119
Kristallnacht 61, 76

Land, Dr. Charles H. 12
Lee, Ivy 38
Lend-Lease 110
Liliuokalani 137
Lindbergh, Anne Morrow
    42, 44, 87, 139, 147
Lindbergh, Charles and Anne,
    children of 46
Lindbergh, Charles August
    (C. A.) 10-13, 109
Lindbergh, Charles Augustus
    Jr. 41, 47
Lindbergh, Evangeline Land
    12-13, 43, 85
Lindbergh, Land 134
Lindbergh, Reeve
    xiii, 33, 46, 76
Lindbergh, Scott 47
Little Falls
    12, 59, 141-42, 155
"Lucky Lindy" 5-7
Lutheran church 11
Lyman, Lauren D. "Deac" 92

MacArthur, Gen. Douglas
    96, 98
Malinin, Theodore I. 141
Marciel, David J. K. 136
Maui 123-29
Meigs, Merrill C. 103, 106
Moore, Edward 21

Moral Re-Armament (MRA)
  20 and n, 24, 50, 118–19
Morrow, Dwight W.
  38, 44, 56
Mysticism 27–29

National Aeronautics and Space
  Administration (NASA) 106
New Testament 45, 98, 102
New York Times, The 92–93
Newton, James D.
  19–25, 83–84, 118–19
Nicolson, Sir Harold 64

Of Flight and Life
  25, 101–02, 115–17, 119
Only Yesterday 2, 149
Oxford Group
  20 and n, 21–23, 118

Palapala Ho'omau
  Congregational Church
  125, 136
Pan American World Airways
  82, 124
Pechin, Ed and Jeannie
  133, 147
Pennsylvania Railroad 49
Perfusion pump 18, 141
Power, use of 65
Press 79–80, 83–94
Pryor, Samuel F. Jr.
  80, 123–26
Public relations 36, 38, 86, 87
Publicity 4, 79–81

Quality of life
  24, 30, 108, 143, 156

Reader's Digest 18, 24, 67
Religious rejuvenation 24, 119
Rio Rita 37
Robertson Aircraft Corp. 104
Robertson, Cliff 82
Rockefeller Institute for
  Medical Research 18
Rogers, James B. 58
Rogers, Will 2, 3, 47, 53–58
Roosevelt, Franklin D.
  69–74, 110
Russia 112

Sandburg, Carl 73
Scientific materialism 115–118
Smith, Col. Truman 65, 67
South Pacific theater 98
St. Johns, Adela Rogers
  41–42, 79
Standards 48
Stewart, James 2
Style, graceful 104
Supersonic Transport (SST)
  107

Time frontispiece, 18
Tincher, Rev. John M.
  131, 137
Trans World Airlines (TWA)
  60, 131
Trudeau, Garry 89

United Aircraft Corp. 98
USS Memphis 43, 85

Vandenberg, Senator Arthur H.
  112
*Verdienstkreuz der Deutscher
  Adler* 60
Vietnam War 47–48, 80

Wananalua Congregational
    Church 45, 137
Washington, George 48
We 5, 35, 39
Whitehead, Alfred North
    95, 119
Whitman, Alden 6, 93
Willkie, Wendell 69, 109, 124
Wilson, Ambassador Hugh R.
    60-61
Wilson, Woodrow 36
Wright Aeronautical Corp. 85

Ziegfeld, Florenz 37, 57

About the Author

T. Willard Hunter is a newspaper columnist and platform orator living in the college community of Claremont, California, east of Los Angeles. Born in Emmett, Idaho, he grew up in Northfield, Minnesota as the son of a college professor, and was educated at Carleton College, Harvard Law School, and Andover Newton Theological School. His career has included higher education and the Christian ministry, serving colleges and churches in New Hampshire, Minnesota, California, and Hawaii. In the forties and fifties he was an associate of Frank Buchman and served as a staff executive with the Oxford Group/Moral Re-Armament program in Washington D.C., Michigan, and Africa. He is co-author of the official Alcoholics Anonymous statement "AA's Roots in the Oxford Group." A patron of Fourth of July oratory, he was pictured in the 1984 and 1985 editions of the Guinness Book of World Records for his thirty-four hour address at Independence Hall, Philadelphia, in 1982. He has been a recurrent keynote speaker at Will Rogers Days in Claremore, Oklahoma, and Lindbergh related events at Kipahulu, Maui, and Little Falls, Minnesota.

The author is married to the former Mary Louise Merrell of Indianapolis, a homemaker, college personnel administrator, and community volunteer. They have two living sons—a minister in Bellingham, Washington, who works with teachers to motivate children with his music, and a family practice physician who directs a rural health center in Garberville, California. There are four grandchildren.